REVELATION

Daniel J. Harrington

REVELATION

The Book
of the
Risen Christ

New City Press

Published in the United States by New City Press
202 Cardinal Rd., Hyde Park, NY 12538
©1999 Daniel J. Harrington

Cover design by Nick Cianfarani

The cover artwork is entitled "Through the Gate of the Eternal City" and is from the series "Revelation Illustrated" by Pat Marvenko Smith, © 1992. Used with permission. Art prints as well as teaching aids and videos are available. For a free brochure write: Revelation Productions, 1740 Ridgeview Dr., North Huntington, PA 15642, 1-800-327-7330, www.revelationillustrated.com.

Library of Congress Cataloging-in-Publication Data:
    Harrington, Daniel J.
        Revelation : the book of the risen Christ / Daniel J. Harrington.
            p.   cm. -- (Spiritual commentaries)
        Includes bibliographical references.
        ISBN 1-56548-121-6
        1. Bible N.T. Revelation--Commentaries.   I. Title.
    II. Series.
    BS2825.3.H325   1999   99-18778
    228'.077--dc21   CIP

2d printing: August 2001

Printed in Canada

Contents

Dedication

I dedicate this book to the memory of John T. Carmody. We entered the Society of Jesus on the same day in 1958. John left the Society in the 1970s and married Denise Lardner Carmody. They formed an extraordinary couple, dedicated to study, teaching, prayer, and writing. Denise and John invited me to give a Warren Lecture at the University of Tulsa in March 1992. I took as my topic the book of Revelation, and large parts of that lecture form the basis of the first three sections of my introduction here. The full text appeared as "A Catholic Reading of the Book of Revelation," in *New Theology Review* 6 (1993) 53-63. During my visit to Tulsa, John was in remission from the cancer that would eventually take his life in 1995. He knew that he had little time left, and he wanted to spend it by writing about scripture in a way that would make it accessible to ordinary folk and that would help them pray and live a Christian life. We talked about his plans and about the pastoral value of *lectio divina*. That breakfast conversation kindled my own interest in this kind of writing, and has led me to contribute three books to this series.

Introduction

Most of us are afraid of the book of Revelation. Our minds grow numb when we hear all those sevens and twelves, and all those strange titles applied to Jesus—the slain Lamb, the Alpha and Omega, and the bright morning star. There is no lack of people who want to tell us what Revelation really means. And they frighten us even more. The fundamentalists talk about the breakup of the Soviet Union, the United Europe, and the state of Israel. They divide themselves into pre-, post-, and a-millennialists, and pre- and post-tribulationists. The Marxists hold Revelation up as an example of religion offered as an opiate to oppressed and exploited peoples, promising that all their problems will be solved only in the "sweet bye-and-bye." Humanist despisers of Christianity reject Revelation as grotesque and barbaric, full of vengeance and pathology. And biblical scholars love to pile up parallels between Revelation and other ancient works, sometimes adding to the numbness and fears of God's people about Revelation. Most of us make a hasty retreat when someone proposes to tell us what it really means.

Mainline Christians have some exposure to the book of Revelation in the cycle of lectionary readings. In Year C (2001, 2004, 2007, etc.) the epistle readings for the Sundays between Easter and Pentecost are taken from the book of Revelation. In Year II of the weekday cycle (2000, 2002, 2004, etc.) the first reading during the last two weeks of ordinary time is from Revelation. We are exposed to the texts. But they are seldom the topic of homilies. And since we only hear small parts of the book, we quickly lose the thread and with that our interest.

Avoidance is not a good remedy for fear and ignorance. The book of Revelation is part of the Church's scriptures, and we owe it to ourselves as God's people to become familiar with that segment of our religious heritage. At the dawn of the new millennium, some wild statements are being made in the name of the book of Revelation. We ought to find out what the text says. And then as we work through the book out of duty and curiosity, we may discover a rich theological resource regarding Christ and the Church, and an important help to our personal and communal spirituality. That is the hope on which this commentary is based.

Literary Features

The book of Revelation is most obviously an apocalypse. In an apocalypse a seer is granted a revelation (*apokalypsis* in Greek) of the future and/or of the heavenly realm. The book of Daniel is at least in part an apocalypse in the Old Testament. Within the Gospels, Jesus' final discourse (Mk 13, Mt 24–24, Luke 21) is sometimes called the "little apocalypse." The most prominent Jewish apocalypses outside the canon of scripture are the books known as *1 Enoch, 4 Ezra*, and *2 Baruch*. There are apocalyptic elements in many of the Dead Sea scrolls and among early

Christian noncanonical texts (*Apocalypse of Peter, Shepherd of Hermas*).

Yet Revelation is not simply an apocalypse. It is also a book of prophecy: "Blessed is the one who reads aloud . . . this prophetic message" (1:3). In it John the prophet speaks on God's behalf on the basis of what God had shown him about what was, what is, and what is to come. That is what prophecy in the biblical sense means.

Revelation is also a letter in the tradition of early Christian letters known best from Paul. It has an epistolary salutation: "John, to the seven churches in Asia: grace to you and peace . . ." (1:4). Then in chapters 2 and 3 there are seven short letters to various churches in Asia Minor. These in turn preface the more properly apocalyptic chapters that constitute the rest of the book. The whole book was probably intended to be sent around from church to church as a kind of encyclical or circular letter. So we have in Revelation an apocalypse that is a prophecy (see 22:10, 18, 19) in letter-form.

Revelation is an extraordinary piece of literature. Its language and literary style are noteworthy mainly for their poor quality—at least when compared with the more elegant Greek of Luke-Acts and Hebrews. The Greek of Revelation is very Semitic, sounding like a translation from Hebrew or Aramaic (though probably not one in fact) and heavily influenced by the Greek translation of the Old Testament (Septuagint). Whether this style is evidence for John's poor grasp of Greek (it was not his native language) or paradoxically for his mastery of Greek (as the Irish writer James Joyce was a master of English and "played" with it), is a matter of debate among scholars.

11

The literary artistry of the book resides more in the overall structure. The author loves the number "seven." So he gives us seven letters to churches in western Asia Minor (present-day Turkey) in which he both praises and blames the individual communities. Then after a glorious vision of God's heavenly throne room and Christ the Lamb (4:1–5:14), the Lamb opens the seven seals (6:1–8:1), and then angels blow on seven trumpets (8:7–11:19) and pour out seven bowls of wrath (16:1-21). These three septets constitute punishments for rebelliousness against God and warnings to repent. The septets are introduced by scenes of the heavenly court (4:1–5:14; 8:2-6; 15:1-8) and punctuated by reports on the faithful and their struggles against the unholy trinity of Satan, the beast (the Roman emperor), and the false prophet (a local official) (see 13:1-18). The book reaches its climax with God's triumph over Babylon (a code-name for Rome) in chapters 17–18 and the appearance of the new Jerusalem in chapters 21–22. It is possible to see the new Jerusalem (21:9–22:5) as the climax and result of a series of seven eschatological (end-time) events: the parousia of the Word of God (19:11-16), the last battle (19:17-21), the binding of Satan (20:1-3), the millennium (20:4-6), the defeat of Satan (20:7-10), the last judgment (20:11-15), and the new heaven and the new earth (22:1-8). And there are seven beatitudes ("Blessed is the one who . . . are they who . . .") scattered throughout the letter (1:3; 14:13; 16:15; 19:9; 20:6; 22:7, 14). Seven letters, seven seals, seven trumpets, seven bowls, seven eschatological events, and seven beatitudes—these series of sevens provide the basic structural principle of the book.

12

The literary artistry also resides in the images used in the book. Once we get into chapter 4, the images come fast and furious: the heavenly throne room, Christ the Lamb, the heavenly choirs, the four horsemen, the 144,000 marked with the seal, and so forth. The effect is sometimes sensory overload.

John's use of biblical imagery has been aptly called the "rebirth of images." This means that John took images from the Hebrew Bible as well as from the Jewish apocalyptic tradition and even from pagan mythology and gave them new meaning and dynamism by placing them in the context of the Christ-event. There are hundreds of allusions to the Jewish Scriptures but no direct quotations (as in Matthew's formula quotations, "All this took place to fulfill . . ."). The images may be old and familiar, but John always makes us look at them from new and fresh angles.

Revelation was and is an oral piece: "Blessed is the one who reads aloud, and blessed are they who listen . . ." (1:3). It is a liturgical piece, intended for community reading, not solitary study. When read in a group today and under the proper circumstances, its impact is far more powerful than when read in isolation. The words assault our minds and force us to draw pictures with our imaginations. We get into the dynamic of the story and imagine what this or that character may look like as they do this or that action.

There is an old debate about the movement of the text: Is it linear (showing steady progress toward a climax), or repetitive (recapitulating the same events under different forms)? Those who hold that the movement is linear contend that the seven seals, seven trumpets, and seven bowls move directly forward to the seven end-time events issu-

13

ing in the new Jerusalem. Those who hold that Revelation is recapitulation say that these series are just variant ways of describing what is set out in the "little apocalypse" of Mark 13 and parallels. In fact, neither linear progress nor recapitulation accounts for all the data in Revelation. There is surely some linear progress moving from the present state of the churches in Asia Minor to the new Jerusalem. But John paces the progress by interrupting the septets and injecting visions of hope in the midst of the destruction visited upon rebellious humankind and the elements of nature befouled by sin and rebellion. The fact that there is both linear progress and recapitulation is probably part of John's literary artistry.

Historical Features

The author of Revelation was named John (1:1, 4, 9), a common Jewish name of the time. He makes no claim to be John the Apostle or John the Evangelist, and there is little (though some) connection between Revelation and the Johannine Gospel and Epistles. This John had been exiled to Patmos, a small island about fifty miles south of Ephesus. His exile was the result of his evangelistic activities on behalf of "God's word and . . . testimony to Jesus" (1:9). He knew the pastoral situations of the seven churches addressed in chapters 2 and 3 and had probably been active in them. He tells us that his vision took place on the Lord's Day (1:10)—most likely Sunday. Given his profound knowledge of the Jewish Scriptures and apocalyptic traditions, and given the Semitic character of his Greek, it appears that John was of Jewish origin.

The second-century Christian writer Irenaeus dated the composition of Revelation to "near the end of Domitian's reign" (*Against Heresies* 5.30.3). Since Domitian reigned as Roman emperor between A.D. 81 and 96, that comment places the book's writing around A.D. 95 or 96. The occasion for the book's composition was a persecution, or at least the threat of a persecution, directed against the churches of western Asia Minor: Ephesus, Smyrna, Pergamum, Thyatira, Sardis, Philadelphia, and Laodicea.

The persecution was a response to the Christians' refusal to participate in civil religious rituals that portrayed the Roman emperor as a god and celebrated the goddess Roma. We probably should not imagine an officially sponsored imperial religious program or an empire-wide systematic persecution of Christians. Both the cults and the persecution were local and confined to western Asia Minor—at least insofar as they concerned the book of Revelation.

In fact, the cult of the goddess Roma—a personification of the city of Rome and its empire—had deep roots in the western Asian cult of the Great Mother. The deification of the emperor was a revival of the divine honors paid to Alexander the Great and long before him to the Pharaohs of Egypt and other so-called divine kings. The emperor Domitian liked to be called "my Lord and my God" and did nothing to discourage the cult. A certain unnamed local official in western Asia Minor seems to have been an enthusiastic promoter of the emperor- and Roma-cults. In Revelation this official is described as follows: "Then I saw another beast come up out of the earth; it had two horns like a lamb's but spoke like a dragon. It wielded all the au-

15

thority of the first beast in its sight and made the earth and its inhabitants worship the first beast" (13:11-12).

The language of Revelation would have been clear enough to its first readers. Any local Roman official who picked it up and read it would have quickly understood its (dangerous) political message. God and Christ the Lamb are celebrated in terms that were being applied to the emperor. Supporters of Rome and the goddess Roma cult would surely have understood the parody in chapters 17 and 18, where the great city Babylon/Rome is portrayed as a prostitute seated upon "seven hills" (17:9—the seven hills of Rome). All readers—Christian and non-Christian alike—would have grasped the implications of the cry "Fallen, fallen is Babylon the great" (18:2) hailing its replacement by the "new Jerusalem, coming down out of heaven from God" (21:2). We know a great deal about the historical situation of the book of Revelation.

Despite what we know about the book's original setting and its basic message, much remains difficult and obscure. This is due in large part to the conventions of Jewish apocalyptic literature. Revelation must be read alongside the book of Daniel, the great Jewish apocalypses (*1 Enoch, 4 Ezra, 2 Baruch*), and the Dead Sea scrolls. These works supply much of the language and literary conventions found in Revelation. And remember that these apocalypses all seek to describe the transcendent God and future events. Simple expository prose is not adequate to fully describe God, the heavenly court, and the cosmic events surrounding the end of "this age" and breaking-in of "the age to come." The apocalyptists could describe these figures and events only with the help of images and symbols. And so the apocalypses abound in pictures of the

16

heavenly throne room, grotesque figures with animal features, gigantic angels, numerical series, calculations and measurements, cosmic battle scenes, earthquakes and lightning storms, and judgment scenes.

Apocalyptic has been called the "mother of Christian theology." Its language, imagery, and modes of communication were available and familiar to early Christians, especially to those of Jewish origin. When they found themselves threatened by persecution, it is not surprising that they would express themselves in an apocalypse.

The core of Christian faith, then as now, is the death and resurrection of Jesus. In the Jewish apocalypses resurrection was an end-time event. In Jesus, according to the early Christians, that sequence of end-time events has already been inaugurated by the resurrection of Jesus. The book of Revelation is a Christian apocalypse. It is the book of the risen Jesus. As the Lamb of God who was slain (see 5:6) the risen Jesus is the focus of Christian hope. As "King of kings and Lord of lords" (19:16) the risen Jesus will bring vindication and victory to his faithful followers.

Theological Features

The message intended by John and grasped by the first readers of Revelation is basically clear. Through the death and resurrection of Jesus, God's victory over human rebelliousness and sin has been already achieved. Therefore in the midst of persecution, exile, and even death by martyrdom, those addressed should hold fast to their Christian faith. The persecutors in the form of the Roman emperor and his officials as well as Roma herself will be destroyed. After a difficult period of testing, God and his Messiah

17

will triumph, and all creation will finally acknowledge their lordship in the new Jerusalem with the new heaven and the new earth. Stated in this outline form, John's message is very much like that of the Lord's Prayer (Mt 6:9-13; Lk 11:2-4) in which we ask that God's kingdom may finally come and that in the process of its coming God may sustain us and guard us. John's theological message is mainline early Christian theology and has many parallels in Paul's letters and the Gospels.

The approach taken in this commentary is historical. It contends that John referred to events of his own time and place—the late first century A.D. in western Asia Minor. It views John's work as a symbolic history of contemporary events and an imaginative portrayal of the end of "this age" or "this world." I do not regard Revelation as a detailed forecast of future events. How God brings about the kingdom is in God's hands. And yet I also do not regard Revelation as mere history, as something to be left in the first century and read only by historians of antiquity. In interpreting Revelation there is a middle ground between historicism ("it speaks only about them in the past") and fundamentalism ("it speaks directly about us today"). This reading of Revelation contends that the book speaks to us, not directly about us and not solely about the past. The fact that we still read Revelation in the context of Church liturgies today makes that very point: Revelation speaks to us.

What does it say to us? Revelation is the book of the risen Lord. The events it describes take place after the passion, death, and resurrection of Jesus. The Jesus whom we encounter in Revelation is the risen Jesus—Jesus after Easter, Jesus as he is today. In his first encounter with

John the seer, the risen Jesus identifies himself as "the first and the last, the one who lives" (1:17-18). The "first"—Jesus as God's Wisdom existed before creation, and his resurrection inaugurates the great process of redemption. The "last"—Jesus as the eternal one will exist after the world as we know it ceases to be. The "one who lives"—this same Jesus who died on Good Friday and was raised on Easter Sunday is now alive forever.

In John's first vision of the heavenly court in chapters 4 and 5 he sees the risen Jesus as the Lamb that "seemed to have been slain" (5:6). He sees the risen Jesus in the heavenly throne room—in glory, surrounded by light and splendor, with all kinds of wonderful creatures proclaiming the majesty of God and the worthiness of the Lamb. To early Christian imagination the heavenly throne room would have looked like the court of the Roman emperor. But here the center of attention is the Lamb that was slain, not the Roman emperor. The one who died a criminal's death on the cross at Roman hands is the one whose power and riches, wisdom and strength, honor and glory, and praise last forever. What the Roman emperors and their supporters ambitioned but failed to achieve, the risen Jesus now enjoys in fullness (see 5:12-13).

The last title applied to Jesus in Revelation is the "bright morning star" (22:16; see Nm 24:17). For people in New Testament times the morning star was Venus, the planet that shines more brightly than anything else in the morning sky. It was a symbol of victory, of preeminence, of brilliance. To call Jesus the "bright morning star" was to refer to his resurrection, his vindication, and restoration to life. So from start to finish Revelation is the book of the risen Lord.

Revelation is also the book of the Easter community. What is said about the Church in Revelation is said from the perspective of Easter. The resurrection of Jesus was the first step in the series of end-time events. The victory has already been won; vindication is sure; and the righteous will be rewarded and the wicked will be punished. Easter gave the early Christians a sense of hope and confidence. They knew what God was doing.

And yet Easter faith did not blind John to the grim realities of his present. There were serious problems within the seven communities addressed in chapters 2 and 3: the waning of zeal, opposition from deviant Christians and from the local Jewish community, acceptance of pagan customs and participating in pagan civil religious rituals, and lukewarmness. These people were in the midst of a great crisis of conscience: whether they could or should participate in civil religious rituals that honored the Roman emperor as a god. They were suffering slander and the threat of persecution, and at least in some cases death through martyrdom. What allowed them to carry on in hope and confidence was their Easter faith.

They carried on because they believed in the resurrection of Jesus. In chapter 7 John recounts his vision of the heavenly throne room. He saw a large crowd of people dressed in long white robes and holding palm branches—both signs of victory. They stood before God's throne and Christ the Lamb. One of the elders explains that these people have survived the "great distress" (7:14). They have given their witness and remained faithful, and now their sufferings are over. From now on their life will be the worship of God, sharing the glory of the risen Lord, and praising and loving God.

The link between the grim realities of the present and the glorious future is the resurrection of Jesus. His resurrection is the ground, the basis for all resurrection hope. If Christians remain faithful, they will share the glory of eternity with Christ the Lamb. His resurrection means that our resurrection is possible also.

For those who believe in the resurrection of Jesus, the book of Revelation is not an opiate. Nor is it violent or vengeful. The great battle scenes prepared for in some detail disappear in a verse or two, precisely because in Jesus' resurrection all battles against sin and death have already been won. Evildoers call down God's punishments upon themselves, and these punishments are intended to lead them to repentance. Some texts may imply a universal salvation (see 5:13; 15:4; 21:24), though other texts apparently do not (see 14:9-10; 20:11-15). Whereas to nonbelievers the proclamation of Jesus' resurrection and the hope attached to it can seem to be an opiate, to believers his resurrection makes ours not only a possibility but also a reality.

Revelation and Spirituality

The basic aim of this commentary is to help people overcome their fears about the book of Revelation, and to find in it a resource for their personal and communal spirituality. The exposition that follows is intended to open up the riches of the book by showing forth its literary, historical, and theological dimensions. I do not understand everything in Revelation, and I doubt that anyone else does. But much in the book (I hope to show) is quite accessible.

The book of Revelation is part of the Christian canon of holy scripture. Although there was some debate in the first

Christian centuries about whether it belonged in the canon, it surely has been a solid part of the canon since the fourth century. To neglect Revelation is to neglect a substantial portion of the Christian heritage.

And yet to base a spirituality solely on Revelation carries some dangers with it. It is enough to recall the "David Koresh" episode in Waco, Texas, with its tragic consequences of a foolish reading of Revelation. The obvious danger is borne out by the long series of false identifications of various characters (the beast, the false prophet, etc.) and events (earthquakes, hail storms, etc.) with figures and happenings in current history. Eventually some such identifications may prove to be correct. But enormous amounts of harm have been done by those who have claimed to understand these figures and events in terms of current events. How God will bring about the fullness of the kingdom must be left in the hands of God. We need not look to Revelation for an exact and literal forecast of the future.

According to Revelation (and the other New Testament writings), it is a divine prerogative and task to bring about the kingdom of God, when and how God sees fit. In the meantime, we humans are asked to be faithful witnesses to God and Jesus Christ (the Lamb). Two dangerous attitudes that can flow even from this correct belief are passivity (expecting God to do everything and therefore doing nothing on one's own) and a vengeful spirit (expecting God to settle one's grievances against real or imagined enemies). Neither attitude is appropriate to a genuine Christian spirituality.

Rather than dwelling on the dangerous and the negative dimensions of Revelation, this volume seeks to be positive and constructive by exploring what contributions Revelation might make to Christian spirituality. I understand spirituality in a broad sense as how one stands before God and relates to others in light of that relationship. A spirituality shaped by the book of Revelation has the following ten characteristics.

Imaginative: Revelation communicates through images, symbols, and visions, not by definitions or linear narratives. It demands the active use of the imagination on the part of its readers.

Biblical: The images, symbols, and visions are expressed almost entirely with the help of the Old Testament. And yet the biblical language and imagery take on new significance in light of the central event in salvation history—Jesus' death and resurrection.

Prophetic: The biblical prophet (in this case, John) speaks God's word to the present and points to what God will do in the future on the basis of God's promises. The prophet's word is one of hope for a new and better future.

Paschal: Revelation is preeminently the book of the slain Lamb and the glorious risen Christ. Its spirituality is rooted in Jesus' death and resurrection.

Marginal: The word of hope based on Jesus' death and resurrection is addressed to and best heard by oppressed and marginal people. The persecuted and imprisoned seem to understand it better than the learned and the socially and economically secure do. And rightly so, since the book was originally addressed to an oppressed minority in the Roman empire.

23

Political: The early Christians addressed in Revelation found themselves in a religious-political conflict about participating in the worship of the Roman emperor and the goddess Roma (the personification of the empire). Their situation raises the issue of conflict between the dictates of Christian conscience and the demands of an intrusive government.

Communal: Throughout Revelation, the focus is not isolated individuals but rather the community of Christian faith. In chapters 2–3 we have a frank accounting of the successes and failures of seven churches. In chapters 4–22 we have advice and encouragement for Christians under pressure. The focus is always the community.

Committed: It is chiefly from Revelation that we derive the idea of martyrdom as Christian witness that is faithful unto death. It is not clear how many Christians actually died in the persecutions envisioned in the book. But its ideal of fidelity under pressure has shaped Christian consciousness ever since.

Suffering: Suffering is the background for the entire book. There are many biblical approaches to suffering: divine discipline, punishment for sin, part of the human condition, mystery, and so forth. Revelation (and the book of Daniel) places the suffering of the righteous community in the framework of the coming kingdom of God—when the righteous will be vindicated, and there will be no more suffering.

Joyful: The joyful spirit that permeates the book is based on the conviction that Jesus' death and resurrection marked the victory of God over evil. Those who bear faithful witness to God and the Lamb share their triumph. Therefore Revelation is full of joyful hymns that celebrate the victory of God and the Lamb. The text has also been the inspiration for great Christian hymns from the Alleluia chorus in Handel's Messiah to "We Shall Overcome."

The exposition of Revelation that follows is based on the *New American Bible* (Revised). It explains the text on the literary, historical, and theological levels. It tries to clarify the literal sense of the text (what the author was saying to his audience in the late first century). It includes references to those Old Testament passages that are essential for understanding the text. At the end of almost every section there are questions for reflection and prayer. These are meant only to suggest how Revelation speaks to us, to put in motion the process of imaginative identification with Revelation through reading, meditation, discussion, prayer, and action.

Revelation is preeminently a work of Christian imagination. As such, it demands an imaginative response from the reader. The traditional way of reading scripture known as *lectio divina* ("spiritual reading") can help. The first step in this method involves reading the text slowly and reverently, always asking "What does the text say?" The exposition provided in this volume can help to answer that question. With Revelation it is particularly important also to engage the senses and the imagination by asking, What do I see? What do I hear? What do I smell? What do I taste? What do I touch?

The second step in *lectio divina* is meditation—in answer to the question, "What does the text say to me?" The third step is prayer, or "What do I want to say to God through this text?" The fourth and final step might be one of contemplation (enjoying the experience of union with God) and/or action, "What should be done in response to the text?" The reflections at the end of each section are designed to facilitate the second, third, and fourth steps. And yet these matters remain very much the territory of those who read and use this book. The goal of this commentary is to help you to think, pray, and act with the aid of the book of Revelation.

I
Prologue and Address

The opening passage identifies the book as a revelation from God, a prophecy, and a letter to seven churches in western Asia Minor. It also introduces the main characters: John the seer, his audience, the risen Christ, and God. The revelation comes from God through Christ to John and his communities. As will become clear, John and his fellow Christians found themselves in great distress and hoped for divine help soon.

Prologue and Address (1:1-8)

¹ The revelation of Jesus Christ, which God gave to him, to show his servants what must happen soon. He made it known by sending his angel to his servant John, ² who gives witness to the word of God and to the testimony of Jesus Christ by reporting what he saw.

³ Blessed is the one who reads aloud and blessed are those who listen to this prophetic message and heed what is written in it, for the appointed time is near.

⁴ John, to the seven churches in Asia: grace to you and peace from him who is and who was and who is to come, and from the seven spirits before his throne, and ⁵ from Jesus Christ, the faithful witness, the firstborn of the dead and ruler of the kings of the earth. To him who loves us and has freed us from our sins by his blood, ⁶ who has made us into a kingdom, priests for his God

and Father, to him be glory and power forever [and ever]. Amen.

⁷ Behold, he is coming amid the clouds,
 and every eye will see him,
 even those who pierced him.
All the peoples of the earth will lament him.
 Yes. Amen.

⁸ "I am the Alpha and the Omega," says the Lord God, "the one who is and who was and who is to come, the almighty."

A prologue serves to introduce the major characters and themes in a work. The first part of the prologue (1:1-2) to the book of Revelation tells us where the revelation came from and what its content is. It came from God through Jesus Christ (by way of an angel) to John the seer. It concerns "what must happen soon"—which is the content of the word of God and testimony of Jesus Christ. John must report this revelation to his fellow Christians. That this is a revelation (*apokalypsis*) is underlined by the verbs "gave . . . show . . . made it known . . . give witness . . . saw."

Then in 1:3 the first of seven beatitudes in the work (see also 14:13; 16:15; 19:9; 20:6; 22:7, 14) declares blessed or happy both the one who reads this prophecy aloud and those who hear it and hold on to it (see Lk 11:28; Jn 12:47). The revelation is a prophecy in the sense that it speaks to the present evil situation and offers hope for a better future. The beatitude assures the readers that the liberation and triumph described in the revelation will come soon ("the appointed time is near").

The address (1:4-8) consists of an epistolary introduction (1:4-5a), a doxology (1:5b-6), a prophecy (1:7), and a divine declaration (1:8).

Besides being an apocalypse (1:1) and a book of prophecy (1:3), Revelation takes the form of a letter addressed by John the seer to seven churches (see also 1:11; 2–3) in the Roman province of Asia (now southwestern Turkey). The usual New Testament letter greeting ("grace to you and peace") is followed by an unusual trinitarian formula. The description of God as "who is and who was and who is to come" echoes Exodus 3:14 ("I am who am"). The "seven spirits before his throne" is more difficult to understand. It is sometimes taken to refer to angels (those of the seven churches) or archangels. Given the prominence of the number seven in Revelation as a symbol of fullness, this may be a way of describing the manifold activities of the one Holy Spirit (see 4:5; 5:6). The titles ascribed to Jesus—the faithful witness (see 3:14), the firstborn of the dead (see Col 1:15, 18; 1 Cor 15:20), and the ruler of the kings of the earth (see Ps 89:28; Is 55:4)—would have given encouragement and confidence to the first readers of Revelation in their struggles.

The doxology ("to him be glory and power") in 1:5b-6 is addressed to the risen Christ. It celebrates Christ's continuing love for humans that has been made manifest in his redeeming death. The formulation ("who . . . has freed us from our sins by his blood") interprets Jesus' death on the cross as a sacrifice that brought about atonement for sins. The new relationship with God that has been made possible through Christ's death ("a kingdom, priests for his God and Father") draws on terms in Exodus 19:6. It attributes to Christians the dignity promised to God's people at Mount Sinai. Within Israel the descendants of Aaron and Levi form a priesthood to care for the proper worship of God. The second text that is echoed here (Is

61:5-6) looks for the day when Israel taken as a whole will form a priesthood for all the nations of the world. According to 1:5b-6, this prophecy is fulfilled through Christ in the royal priesthood formed by his faithful followers (see 5:10; 20:6).

The prophecy in 1:7 (see Mt 24:30) combines the language of Daniel 7:13 ("Behold, he is coming among the clouds") and Zechariah 12:10 ("and every eye will . . . lament him"). The first part applies the description of the "one like a son of man" in Daniel 7 to the coming manifestation of the victorious Christ. The second part looks toward the universal recognition of the risen Lord, even by those responsible for his death ("those who pierced him," see Jn 19:37). The response evoked by the prophecy is an enthusiastic "Yes. Amen."

The divine declaration in 1:8 concerns the nature of the Lord God. He is "the Alpha and the Omega"—the first and last letters of the Greek alphabet; that is, the beginning and the end of all creation. He is declared once more (see 1:4) to be "the one who is and who was and who is to come"; that is, the one who exercises sovereignty over the present, past, and future. So God is rightly called the "almighty"—an expression frequently used of God in the book (see 4:8; 11:17; 15:3; 16:7; 19:6; 21:22).

For Reflection: Imagine yourself as among those who listened to the prophetic message for the first time (see 1:3). How is God described? What titles and images are applied to the risen Christ? What does it mean to have been loved and freed from your sins "by his blood"? How does it feel to be part of "a kingdom, priests for his God and Father"? How might this passage have helped the first readers to interpret their situation? How might it help you to approach God in prayer?

II

The First Vision of the Risen Christ

Revelation is preeminently the book of the risen Christ. And so it is fitting that it takes as a starting point the vision of the risen Christ. In 1:9-11 John the seer describes the circumstances of his vision and the command given to him to write down his vision. Then with the help of biblical images he recounts in 1:12-16 what he saw of the risen Christ. In 1:17-18 the risen Lord identifies himself, and in 1:19 he commands the seer to write what about the past, present, and future has been revealed in his visions. Finally in 1:20 there is mention of the seven churches and their "angels"—which prepares for the letters to the seven churches in chapters 2–3.

The First Vision (1:9-20)

⁹ I, John your brother, who share with you the distress, the kingdom, and the endurance we have in Jesus, found myself on the island called Patmos, because I proclaimed God's word and gave testimony to Jesus. ¹⁰ I was caught up in spirit on the Lord's day and heard behind me a voice as loud as a trumpet, ¹¹ which said, "Write on a scroll what you see and send it to the seven churches: to Ephesus, Smyrna, Pergamum, Thyatira, Sardis, Philadelphia, and Laodicea. ¹² Then I turned to see whose voice it was that spoke to me, and when I turned, I saw

seven gold lampstands [13] and in the midst of the lampstands one like a son of man, wearing an ankle-length robe, with a gold sash around his chest. [14] The hair of his head was as white as wool or as snow, and his eyes were like a fiery flame. [15] His feet were like polished brass refined in a furnace, and his voice was like the sound of rushing water. [16] In his right hand he held seven stars. A sharp two-edged sword came out of his mouth, and his face shone like the sun at its brightest.

[17] When I caught sight of him, I fell down at his feet as though dead. He touched me with his right hand and said, "Do not be afraid. I am the first and the last, [18] the one who lives. Once I was dead, but now I am alive forever and ever. I hold the keys to death and the netherworld. [19] Write down, therefore, what you have seen, and what is happening, and what will happen afterwards. [20] This is the secret meaning of the seven stars you saw in my right hand, and of the seven gold lampstands: the seven stars are the angels of the seven churches, and the seven lampstands are the seven churches.

In 1:9-11 John the seer explains that he has been commanded to write down his vision of the risen Christ for the seven churches of western Asia Minor. There has been a shift in speakers from God (1:8) to John (1:9). The seer claims to be related to his readers by their participation in the present suffering and in God's kingdom. What makes this possible is "endurance" based on faith in the risen Christ. The vision took place on the island of Patmos, some fifty miles south of Ephesus. It was used by the Romans as a penal colony. John was there apparently in exile or under arrest for proclaiming the gospel ("God's word and . . . testimony to Jesus").

The vision itself (1:10) was an ecstatic experience ("caught up in spirit") on a Sunday ("the Lord's day"), which was the weekly commemoration of Jesus' resurrection. It was preceded by the command given in "a voice as loud as a trumpet." The command (1:11) is to write the vision on a papyrus scroll and send it to the seven churches. These local Christian communities were strategically placed in western Asia Minor to serve as communication centers. At each stop on the route new copies of the book could be made, and so the account of John's vision might circulate throughout the region.

The object of John's vision (1:12-16) is the glorious risen Christ. His description is rooted in various biblical texts, and its details appear again in chapters 2–3. The seven golden lampstands (1:12) evoke the descriptions of the lampstand with seven lamps in Zechariah 4:2, and of the candlestick in Exodus 25:31-39. The expression "one like a son of man" (1:13; see Dn 7:13) suggests a more than human figure—an angel, or in this case the glorious risen Christ. The long robe with the golden sash is appropriate to such a magnificent figure, suggesting also his priestly and royal identity. He has the white hair (1:14) of the Ancient of Days (see Dn 7:9), and his eyes are like flames of fire (see Dn 10:6). His feet (1:15) are like polished bronze (see Dn 10:6), and his voice is like "rushing water"—like the voice of God (see Ez 43:2).

That he holds in his right hand (1:16) seven stars (the planets known at the time) indicates the cosmic sovereignty of the risen Christ. His judicial authority is expressed by the sharp two-edged sword (see Is 11:4; Heb 4:12) coming out of his mouth. His word is powerful and works its effect. The glory of his face is expressed by the image of the sun shining at its brightest.

Almost every one of these images in 1:12-16 is based on biblical phrases. But there are no direct quotations, and there are some daring shifts (for example, seven lampstands instead of one, white hair on the one like a son of man rather than on the Ancient of Days). The glory of the risen Christ is such that it can be expressed only through biblical images and allusions. And yet so glorious is the risen Christ that he bursts the conventional boundaries of those images and allusions.

The seer's response (1:17) to his vision of the risen Christ is appropriately one of fear. He is, however, reassured in 1:17b when the speaker identifies himself in terms of the resurrection. He is "the first and the last" (see Is 44:6; 48:12)—a biblical designation of God now applied to the risen Christ. He is also "the one who lives." Despite having died, he now lives forever. Having conquered death, the risen Christ possesses the "keys to death and the netherworld." He can liberate those who have died, because neither death nor the abode of the dead (Sheol, Hades) can resist his power (1:18; see 20:14).

The seer in 1:19 is to write down the revelation that comes from the risen Christ (see 1:1). That revelation consists of the vision of the risen Christ in 1:12-16 ("what you have seen"), the current state of the churches addressed in chapters 2–3 ("what is happening"), and the vision of what is to come in chapter 4 onward ("what will happen afterwards").

The parenthetical explanations of the seven stars in the right hand of the risen Christ (see 1:16) as the guardian "angels" of the seven churches, and of the seven lampstands (see 1:12) as the seven churches in 1:20, prepare for the seven letters that follow. The "angels" are more likely superhuman figures than the human leaders of the churches.

For Reflection: John the seer invites the reader/hearer to see what he saw and to hear what he heard. Imagine yourself sharing the vision with John on Patmos. What do you hear? What do you see? What is the effect of all these images applied to the risen Christ. What significance does the risen Christ have in your outlook and way of acting (your spirituality)?

III

Letters to the Seven Churches

Between John's report of his inaugural vision of the risen Lord (1:9-20) and the various visions and apocalyptic scenarios from chapter 4 onward, there are seven "letters" addressed by the risen Christ to the "angels" of seven churches in western Asia Minor. The letters have five elements: the address, the self-identification of the speaker (with images taken from 1:9-20), a message in which the Christian community is praised and/or blamed, a call to hear, and a promise to the "victor" who shares in the victory of the risen Christ.

Some communities are praised for their fidelity to the gospel and their patient endurance in the face of persecution—even to the point of suffering death. Some communities are blamed for their failures. These communities face various problems—some of their own making (spiritual tepidity), some caused by dissident Christians (who apparently urged accommodation to the local religious and political culture), others apparently stemming from the pressures placed on them by local Roman officials to conform to their civil religion, and still others brought about by the hostility of the local Jewish population.

Careful attention to the letters to the seven churches can teach us much about the original historical setting of the book. These letters can also serve as a guide for churches today as they examine their own conscience and confront what in them is worthy of praise and blame. Moreover, the letters continue to paint a rich picture of the risen Christ and so are a resource for Christology.

To the Church at Ephesus (2:1-7)

> [1] To the angel of the church in Ephesus, write this:
> "The one who holds the seven stars in his right hand, and walks in the midst of the seven gold lampstands says this: [2] 'I know your works, your labor, and your endurance, and that you cannot tolerate the wicked; you have tested those who call themselves apostles but are not, and discovered that they are impostors. [3] Moreover, you have endurance and have suffered for my name, and you have not grown weary. [4] Yet I hold this against you: you have lost the love you had at first. [5] Realize how far you have fallen. Repent, and do the works you did at first. Otherwise, I will come to you and remove your lampstand from its place, unless you repent. [6] But you have this in your favor: you hate the works of the Nicolaitans, which I also hate.
> [7] " 'Whoever has ears ought to hear what the Spirit says to the churches. To the victor I will give the right to eat from the tree of life that is in the garden of God.' "

The first letter in the series illustrates the basic outline followed in all seven letters: the address (2:1a), the identification of the speaker (2:1b), the praise and blame (or encouragement) that the community deserves (2:2-6), the call to hear (2:7a), and the reference to victory (2:7b).

The seer is told to write a letter to the angel of the church in Ephesus (2:1a). The "angel" most likely is not the local bishop but rather the guardian angel assigned to that Christian community, much as the archangel Michael was assigned to be the national protector of God's people Israel (see Dn 10:13, 21; 12:1). Ephesus was the largest and most important of the seven cities addressed. As the capital of the Roman province of Asia, it was a great commercial and religious center. The narratives about Paul's ministry in Ephesus (see Acts 19) indicate some of the varied religious currents and Paul's struggle to plant Christianity there. It soon became a center for the Pauline mission and perhaps the Pauline school. Later traditions make it the place where both John the apostle and Mary the mother of Jesus died.

The speaker is identified as the risen Christ in 2:1b with the help of images taken from the vision in 1:12-16: He "holds the seven stars" (see 1:16), and walks among "the seven gold lampstands" (see 1:12-13). He offers praise (2:2-3), blame (2:4-5), and praise (2:6). The initial praise (2:2-3) points to the Ephesian Christians' hard work and endurance in the midst of suffering. They are commended in particular for their ability to discern who the false apostles are and not to tolerate them. Those who "call themselves apostles but are not" (2:2) are perhaps best equated with Nicolaitans mentioned in 2:6.

The Ephesian Christians are blamed in 2:4-5 because they "have lost the love you had at first"—probably love within the community, though possibly also including love for God and zeal toward outsiders. The remedy proposed is a process of re-conversion: recognizing the fall, repenting, and returning to former good works. They are praised again in 2:6 because they share the risen Christ's hatred for the "works of the Nicolaitans" (2:6). Who these people were is not entirely clear. Perhaps they are the same as those who are criticized in 2:14-15 and 2:20-23 below. Only the (common) name would connect them with Nicolaus, the proselyte of Antioch, who is mentioned in Acts 6:5.

The call to hear (2:7a), which is familiar from the Synoptic Gospels (see Mk 4:9, 23; etc.), links the risen Christ with the Holy Spirit and makes them one in addressing the churches (the Spirit of Christ). To the "victor" or conqueror (2:7b)—one who has remained faithful even to the point of martyrdom—is promised eternal life. The image of the tree of life in the garden of God evokes a return to and a perfection of the picture of paradise in Genesis 2. The victory won by the risen Christ—the victor or conqueror par excellence—has rendered void and overcome the banishment from paradise imposed on Adam and Eve as the result of their sin (see Gn 3:23).

For Reflection: The report on the church at Ephesus is mixed—both praise and blame. The Ephesian Christians are praised for their hard work and endurance for the sake of the gospel, and especially for resisting false apostles and the Nicolaitans—perhaps Christians who counseled cooperation with local Roman officials and participation in civil religious rituals. They are blamed because they have somehow lost the love that they had for one another and for God. Without that love they may not continue to resist those who seek to lead them astray. Imagine yourself as part of a community whose love is waning. What are the signs? What must be done? Is the process of recognition, repentance, and return a realistic method for reviving the spirit of love within the community?

To the Church at Smyrna (2:8-11)

⁸ To the angel of the church in Smyrna, write this:

"The first and the last, who once died but came to life, says this: ⁹ 'I know your tribulation and poverty, but you are rich. I know the slander of those who claim to be Jews and are not, but rather are members of the assembly of Satan. ¹⁰ Do not be afraid of anything that you are going to suffer. Indeed, the devil will throw some of you into prison, that you may be tested, and you will face an ordeal for ten days. Remain faithful until death, and I will give you the crown of life.

¹¹ " 'Whoever has ears ought to hear what the Spirit says to the churches. The victor shall not be harmed by the second death.' "

The second letter is addressed (2:8a) to the angel of the church at Smyrna, a port city (modern Izmir) about thirty miles north of Ephesus. Its success as a commercial center may provide the context for the reference to the Christian community's poverty in 2:9. The presence of a temple dedicated to the goddess Roma may help to explain the imprisonment and possible martyrdom facing the Christians there (see 2:10). The speaker is once more the risen Christ, identified in 2:8b with images from the inaugural vision as "the first and the last" (see 1:17) and as the one "who once died but came to life" (see 1:18a).

The message proper (2:9-10) first refers in general terms to the "tribulation and poverty" (2:9a) of the Christian community at Smyrna, perhaps the result of its unwillingness to participate in the local civil religious rituals. The risen Christ assures them that, despite their external circumstances, they are in fact "rich" in faith and the Spirit (see 2 Cor 6:10; Jas 2:5).

It appears that the local Jewish community (see 2:9b) played a role in the plight of the Smyrnean Christians. The Romans recognized the peculiar character of the Jewish people and granted them exemptions that allowed them to practice their religion without compromise. Thus it is likely that Jews were officially exempted from the more offensive aspects of the emperor cult and the worship of the goddess Roma. From the perspective of the Jews at Smyrna, the local Christians—many of whom may have been Jews by birth—were not really Jews and should not be granted the exemptions given to Jews. Moreover, the Jews at Smyrna probably aided and encouraged the persecution of the local Christians. From the perspective of John the seer, the local Jews were not Jews at all, since Jewish Christians like himself represented the true Israel. Therefore the local Jews in his view were imposters and constituted the "assembly (or, synagogue) of Satan." This sentence provides a window onto the complex social dynamics at work behind the text of Revelation.

The risen Lord in 2:10 counsels trust in the midst of the sufferings that are to come. These sufferings include imprisonment and even martyrdom ("until death"). By attributing these sufferings to "the devil" he situates them in the context of the cosmic struggle between Christ and Satan. Although the time of imprisonment (before trial?) may be short ("for ten days"), there is at the end the real possibility of martyrdom. To those who suffer for the sake of the gospel the risen Christ promises "the crown of life." Just as a crown was granted to the victor in an athletic contest, so the faithful Christian will be granted the fullness of life with the risen Christ.

The call to hear (2:11a) follows the usual pattern (see 2:7a). The "victor" saying (2:11b) renews the promise of eternal life with the risen Christ (the true victor) by reference to the "second death"—the eternal death that sinners receive as their final punishment (see 20:6, 14-15; 21:8). Those who remain faithful in the present trials will escape the second death.

For Reflection: The letter to the Christians at Smyrna offers neither praise nor blame, but rather encouragement in the face of actual and impending persecution. The community there already faces hostility from the local pagan and Jewish populations. And it can expect a more systematic persecution that may issue in martyrdom for many. In this context the letter offers hope based on the resurrection of Jesus. The "one who once died but came to life" (2:8b) promises to those who remain faithful the "crown of life" (2:10b) and escape from the "second death" (2:11b). Imagine yourself as part of a Christian community suffering persecution (and there are many around the world!). How might faith in the risen Christ help you to understand what is happening and to resist the persecutors by remaining faithful to your principles?

To the Church at Pergamum (2:12-17)

¹²To the angel of the church in Pergamum, write this:

"The one with the sharp two-edged sword says this:
¹³ 'I know that you live where Satan's throne is, and yet you hold fast to my name and have not denied your faith in me, not even in the days of Antipas, my faithful witness, who was martyred among you, where Satan lives. ¹⁴ Yet I have a few things against you. You have

43

some people there who hold to the teaching of Balaam, who instructed Balak to put a stumbling block before the Israelites: to eat food sacrificed to idols and to play the harlot. [15] Likewise, you also have some people who hold to the teaching of [the] Nicolaitans. [16] Therefore, repent. Otherwise, I will come to you quickly and wage war against them with the sword of my mouth.

[17] " 'Whoever has ears ought to hear what the Spirit says to the churches. To the victor I shall give some of the hidden manna; I shall also give a white amulet upon which is inscribed a new name, which no one knows except the one who receives it.' "

Pergamum, about fifteen miles from the Mediterranean Sea and forty-five miles north of Smyrna, was important as a center of pagan worship. In particular, it was a center for the cult of the healer god Asclepius whose symbol was a serpent, and perhaps thus related to Satan (see 12:9). Even more important is the fact that Pergamum was a leader in promoting the cult of the emperor and of Roma from the early days of first century A.D. And so on both counts Pergamum could be called "Satan's throne" and the place "where Satan lives" in 2:13. The description of the risen Christ in 2:12b as "the one with the sharp two-edged sword" takes up what was said in the inaugural vision (see 1:17) and prepares for what is said in the body of the letter (see 2:16).

The body of the message first (2:13) praises the Christians at Pergamum for remaining faithful to Christ despite the strength of paganism, especially in resisting worship of the emperor and of Roma. How faithful they were is illustrated by the martyr named Antipas. Nothing is known about him apart from what is said here. He is said to have remained faithful to Christ to the point of being killed. In other words, his fidelity as a witness (*martys*) led to his death by martyrdom (*martyria*).

The blame assigned to the church at Pergamum in 2:14-16 concerns the presence there of some Christians who were apparently willing to participate in pagan worship and encouraged others to do so: "to eat food sacrificed to idols and to play the harlot" (2:14). The latter image most likely refers not to sexual immorality but rather (as frequently in the Old Testament) to idolatry. The practice of eating "food sacrificed to idols" (eating meat blessed first in the name of pagan gods) is discussed at length by Paul in 1 Corinthians 8–10 (who recommends some flexibility and pastoral sensitivity). Here the attitude recommended to the Christians of western Asia Minor is one of absolute rejection. Thus one can suppose that the Nicolaitans (see 2:15; also 2:6) were proposing some kind of accommodation that would allow Christian participation in pagan rituals. Their attitude is compared in 2:14 to the pagan prophet Balaam who directed King Balak (see Nm 31:16) to entice Israel into the sin of fornication. The expression "likewise, you also" in 2:15 refers to the presence of these same false teachers at Ephesus (see 2:6), rather than to two kinds of false teachers in 2:14 and 2:15, respectively. In 2:16 the risen Lord commands repentance and warns that without it he will condemn them at the judgment or destroy them by force—depending on whether "the sword of my mouth" is taken figuratively (the word of the risen Lord) or literally (see 19:15).

The usual call to hear (2:17a) is followed by another promise to the victor (2:17b). The "hidden manna" (see Ps 78:24-25; Ex 16:32-36) will sustain God's people while they abstain from "food sacrificed to idols" (2:14). The white stone inscribed with a new name is more puzzling. It may refer to a positive verdict at God's judgment and/or an amulet or "ticket" admitting the faithful to the heavenly banquet. The "new name" may be that of Christ or of God written in a way that is distinctive for each faithful witness.

For Reflection: Living in a great center of pagan religious activity, the Christians at Pergamum were exposed to temptation from both the outside and the inside. According to 2:13 they had thus far resisted denying their Christian faith to outsiders, even to the point of death in the case of Antipas. And yet, according to 2:14-15, they also faced a threat within the Christian community from those who counseled accommodation to and participation in pagan rituals. Can you imagine how the Nicolaitans argued for their position? What side would you have taken?

To the Church at Thyatira (2:18-29)

¹⁸ To the angel of the church in Thyatira, write this:
"The Son of God, whose eyes are like a fiery flame and whose feet are like polished brass, says this: ¹⁹ 'I know your works, your love, faith, service, and endurance, and that your last works are greater than the first. ²⁰ Yet I hold this against you, that you tolerate the woman Jezebel, who calls herself a prophetess, who teaches and misleads my servants to play the harlot and to eat food sacrificed to idols. ²¹ I have given her time to repent, but she refuses to repent of her harlotry. ²² So I will cast her on a sickbed and plunge those who commit adultery with her into intense suffering unless they repent of her works. ²³ I will also put her children to death. Thus shall all the churches come to know that I am the

searcher of hearts and minds and that I will give each of you what your works deserve. ²⁴ But I say to the rest of you in Thyatira, who do not uphold this teaching and know nothing of the so-called deep secrets of Satan: on you I will place no further burden, ²⁵ except that you must hold fast to what you have until I come.

> ²⁶ " 'To the victor, who keeps to my ways until the end,
> I will give authority over the nations.
> ²⁷ He will rule them with an iron rod.
> Like clay vessels will they be smashed,
> ²⁸ just as I received authority from my Father. And
> to him I will give the morning star.
> ²⁹ Whoever has ears ought to hear what the Spirit
> says to the churches.' "

Thyatira, about forty miles southeast of Pergamum, was known as a commercial center (see Acts 16:14) with many trade guilds. These guilds organized common meals at which food blessed in the name of this or that god was served. While some local Christians saw no problem in participating in such feasts, the risen Christ in 2:20 regards this practice as idolatry. The description of the risen Christ as the Son of God in 2:18b prepares for the extensive use of Psalm 2 in 2:26-28. The references to his eyes like a fiery flame and his feet like polished brass depend on details in the inaugural vision (1:14b-15a).

The body of the message consists of praise (2:19), blame (2:20-23), and words of warning and encouragement (2:24-25). The praise (2:19) suggests a community that displays the proper Christian virtues and is making progress in them. The blame (2:20-23) focuses on a woman prophet who is judged to be leading the community astray. In 2:20 she is called "Jezebel," after the pagan wife of King Ahab of Israel, who introduced the worship of

47

foreign gods into Israel (see 1 Kgs 16:31; 2 Kgs 9:22). The Thyatiran Christians are blamed for tolerating this self-styled prophet, who in fact was leading them into idolatry. The description of her teaching ("to play the harlot and to eat food sacrificed to idols") in 2:20 suggests a relationship to the Nicolaitans (see 2:6, 14-15). That this teaching involved literal sexual immorality is not certain. The sexual imagery may be metaphorical (= idolatry). Her teaching more likely gave permission to Christians to participate in trade guild banquets at which food dedicated to pagan gods was served.

Thus far the woman prophet had refused to disavow her teaching and repent, and so she and her followers are threatened with sickness and even death as punishment (2:21-23a). The risen Lord describes himself as "the searcher of hearts and minds"—a title traditionally applied to God in the Old Testament (see Jer 11:20; 17:10; 20:12; Ps 7:10), and as the one who rewards and punishes according to one's works (see 22:12). To those Christians at Thyatira who did not follow the woman prophet's teaching, the Lord has no further commands—only a warning to remain faithful to what they have already received until his return (see 22:20). The characterization of the woman prophet's teachings as "the deep secrets of Satan" probably alludes in a sarcastic way to her appeal to possess an esoteric knowledge that allowed participation in pagan rituals. The point here is that, rather than coming from God (as she claims), this alleged knowledge comes from Satan.

The closing of the letter places the "victor" saying (2:26-28) before the call to hear (2:29). The "victor" saying promises those who remain faithful to Christ's coming (see 2:25) a share in his authority as the Messiah. The words are taken from Psalm 2, a psalm used originally in the coronation of ancient Israel's kings and then understood to refer to the Anointed One of God (the Messiah). As God's Son, the Messiah receives authority over the nations and has the power to subjugate and destroy them (see Ps 2:7-9). The "victor" is also promised a share in the risen Christ's victory over death as symbolized by the "morning star" (see 22:16).

For Reflection: Most readers focus on the negative (admittedly fascinating) "Jezebel" section of the letter to the church at Thyatira and pass over the positive dimensions of Christian life that are also sketched here. The list of virtues in 2:19 ("love, faith, service, and endurance") should characterize every sound Christian community. And 2:26-28 promises those who remain faithful a share in the authority of the Messiah/Son of God and in the risen Christ's victory over death. Do these virtues characterize your faith-community? Do you think of yourself as sharing in the risen Christ's victory and authority?

To the Church at Sardis (3:1-6)

[1] To the angel of the church in Sardis, write this:
"The one who has the seven spirits of God and the seven stars says this: I know your works, that you have the reputation of being alive, but you are dead. [2] Be watchful and strengthen what is left, which is going to die, for I have not found your works complete in the sight of my God. [3] Remember then how you accepted and heard; keep it, and repent. If you are not watchful, I will come like a thief, and you will never know at what hour I will come upon you. [4] However, you have a few

people in Sardis who have not soiled their garments; they will walk with me in white, because they are worthy.

⁵ " 'The victor will thus be dressed in white, and I will never erase his name from the book of life but will acknowledge his name in the presence of my Father and of his angels.

⁶ " 'Whoever has ears ought to hear what the Spirit says to the churches.' "

Sardis, about thirty miles southeast of Thyatira, was famous for its wealth under King Croesus ("as rich as Croesus") in the sixth century B.C. Thought to be impregnable, it was captured by surprise attacks first in Croesus' time (546 B.C.) and then by Antiochus III (214 B.C.). It suffered heavy damage from an earthquake in A.D. 17 but was quickly rebuilt. It had a large Jewish population. The description of the risen Christ in 3:1b combines elements from 1:4 ("the seven spirits of God") and 1:16 ("the seven stars").

The body of the letter (3:1c-4) contains both blame (3:1c-3) and praise (3:4). Perhaps alluding to the recent rebuilding of Sardis after the earthquake, the risen Lord castigates the church there for being dead while having only the fame of being alive (3:1c). Perhaps alluding to Sardis having been captured by surprise attacks and damaged by an earthquake, he urges the Christians there to be vigilant (3:2). He contrasts their present imperfection (3:2) and the fervor with which they first accepted the gospel (3:3), and urges them to rekindle that fervor. Like the surprise attacks of the past and the more recent earthquake, the coming of the risen Christ will be sudden and unexpected—like the coming of a thief (see 1 Thes 5:2, 4;

Mt 24:43-44; Lk 12:39-40). Since the precise time of Christ's coming is not known, one should always be on guard and behave as if he is to come at the very next moment.

The praise in 3:4 is reserved for those few Christians at Sardis "who have not soiled their garments"—most likely a reference to their refusal to participate in worship of the emperor and the goddess Roma. Because of their fidelity, these persons will share the glory of the risen Lord: "they will walk with me dressed in white."

As in the preceding letter, the "victor" saying (3:5) comes before the call to hear (3:6). The victor is promised a share in the glory of the risen Lord ("dressed in white") and a place in "the book of life" (see Ex 32:32-33; Ps 69:29)—the list of those who are to share the fullness of God's kingdom. The promise that the risen Lord will acknowledge such faithful witnesses before God and the angels appears also in Mt 10:32-33.

For Reflection: The picture that emerges from the report on the church at Sardis is one of complacency. Though a few Christians there are praised for their fidelity, most are accused of only seeming to be alive and of still being far from perfection. The risen Lord urges them to recapture their first fervor and to live in a state of constant watchfulness in hope of the Lord's coming. Their problems appear to have arisen not so much from an organized Christian movement (the Nicolaitans and "Jezebel") or from the local Jewish community or even from the Roman officials, but rather from their own complacency. Do you see signs of complacency in your own faith-community? How might the risen Lord's advice in 3:1-6 help to combat such complacency?

To the Church at Philadelphia (3:7-13)

⁷ To the angel of the church in Philadelphia, write this:
"The holy one, the true,
  who holds the key of David,
  who opens and no one shall close,
  who closes and no one shall open,
  says this:
⁸ "'I know your works (behold I have left an open door before you, which no one can close). You have limited strength, and yet you have kept my word and have not denied my name. ⁹ Behold, I will make those of the assembly of Satan who claim to be Jews and are not, but are lying, behold I will make them come and fall prostrate at your feet, and they will realize that I love you. ¹⁰ Because you have kept my message of endurance I will keep you safe in the time of trial that is going to come to the whole world to test the inhabitants of the earth. ¹¹ I am coming quickly. Hold fast to what you have, so that no one may take your crown.
  ¹² "'The victor I will make into a pillar in the temple of my God, and he will never leave it again. On him I will inscribe the name of my God and the name of the city of my God, the new Jerusalem, which comes down out of heaven from my God, as well as my new name.
  ¹³ "'Whoever has ears ought to hear what the Spirit says to the churches.'"

Philadelphia, about thirty miles southeast of Sardis, was destroyed by the earthquake of A.D. 17 and rebuilt with Roman help. Since the emperor Tiberius was instrumental in the rebuilding, the city was renamed

Neo-Caesarea, which may explain the motifs of building and "name" in 3:12. The first two adjectives applied in 3:7 to the risen Christ ("the holy one, the true") are also applied to God in 6:10. The description in the rest of 3:7, though based on 1:18 ("I hold the keys to death and the netherworld"), is ultimately based on Isaiah 22:22, which appears in Isaiah with reference to Eliakim as chief steward and gatekeeper for the royal house of David. Just as Eliakim allowed or prohibited entrance in David's household at the old Jerusalem, so the risen Christ allows or prohibits entrance into the new Jerusalem. (In Matthew 16:19 the keys of the kingdom of heaven are given to Peter as the representative of Christ.)

The message to the church at Philadelphia (3:8-11) contains praise (3:8) and promises (3:9-11), and no blame. In 3:8 the Philadelphian Christians are praised for their fidelity to the "word" and "name" of Christ, despite their small number. Their good works constitute an "open door" for others to enter, in the sense that their example presents a motive for others to enter the church (see 1 Cor 16:9; 2 Cor 2:12; Acts 14:27).

From 3:9 it is clear that the instigators of the opposition to the Christians at Philadelphia were from the local Jewish community (as at Smyrna, see 2:9). The hostile Jewish community is again named the "synagogue of Satan" (as opposed to their claim to be the "synagogue of the Lord," see Nm 16:3; 20:4), and their identity as Jews is questioned (since the church is now regarded as the true Israel). Nevertheless, the risen Christ promises a reversal or conversion even on the part of the hostile Jewish community in response to the Christian community's good example of fidelity to Christ. Using the motif of the Gentiles coming to join Israel in the book of Isaiah (see 45:14; 49:23; 60:14), the risen Lord promises that the synagogue will eventually join the church as the risen Christ's beloved.

In 3:10-11 the risen Christ also promises as a reward for the Philadelphian Christians' fidelity in the present his future protection in the world-wide testing about to come. Thus he promises what is sought in the Lord's Prayer: "and do not subject us to the final test, but deliver us from the evil one" (Mt 6:13). The Lord will come soon (3:11; see 2:25; 3:3), and Christians must continue in fidelity lest they lose their reward (see 2:10) of the crown of life.

In 3:12 the "victor" is promised to be made into a (metaphorical) "pillar" in the (metaphorical) temple in the new Jerusalem (see 21:22). On that pillar will be inscribed the names of God, the new Jerusalem, and the risen Christ—showing to whom and to what the victor belongs. The building and "name" motifs probably had special significance for the Philadelphian Christians in light of their city's recent history (see above). The concluding call to hear in 3:13 follows the usual format.

For Reflection: The church at Philadelphia receives only praise for its fidelity in the midst of hostility. So powerful an example have they given that, despite their small size, they will attract many others to join them ("an open door"), including the local Jewish community that had been hostile to them. Christianity has always been spread most effectively by the good example shown by Christians—by people who embody the ideals of the Christian faith and show them forth in their lives. Yet even these Christians need to be reminded of the need for constant vigilance on their own part so as to remain faithful themselves. In your experience, what has attracted people to become Christians? Have you ever helped someone become a Christian?

To the Church at Laodicea (3:14-22)

[14]To the angel of the church in Laodicea, write this:

"The Amen, the faithful and true witness, the source of God's creation, says this: [15] 'I know your works; I know that you are neither cold nor hot. I wish you were either cold or hot. [16] So because you are lukewarm, neither hot nor cold, I will spit you out of my mouth. [17] For you say: I am rich and affluent and have no need of anything, and yet do not realize that you are wretched, pitiable, poor, blind, and naked. [18] I advise you to buy from me gold refined by fire so that you may be rich, and white garments to put on so that your shameful nakedness may not be exposed, and buy ointment to smear on your eyes so that you may see. [19] Those whom I love, I reprove and chastise. Be earnest, therefore, and repent.

[20] " 'Behold, I stand at the door and knock. If anyone hears my voice and opens the door, then I will enter his house and dine with him, and he with me. [21] I will give the victor the right to sit with me on my throne, as I myself first won the victory and sit with my Father on his throne.

[22] " 'Whoever has ears ought to hear what the Spirit says to the churches.' "

Laodicea was about forty miles southeast of Philadelphia and about eighty miles east of Ephesus. It was built on the south bank of the Lycus River, ten miles west of Colossae and six miles south of Hierapolis. It was famous as a banking center, as a woolen manufacturing center (for carpets and clothing), and for its medical school. These distinctive features of the city's life are alluded to in 3:17-18. In 3:14b the risen Lord identifies himself as "the Amen" (see Is 65:16), the "faithful and true witness" (see Rv 1:5), and the "source of God's creation"—perhaps a way of talking about Jesus as the Wisdom of God (see Prv 8:22-31; Col 1:16-17; Jn 1:3; Heb 1:2).

The message (3:15-20) contains no praise, only blame (3:15-18) and a call to repent (3:19-20). The Laodicean Christians are blamed for their lack of zeal, their self-satisfaction, and their complacency. Many interpreters find in 3:15-16 allusions to the warm springs of Hierapolis and the cold water of Colossae, in contrast to the tepid water of Laodicea. Just as lukewarm water (or coffee or soda) is distasteful, so the risen Lord finds distasteful the lukewarm piety of the Laodicean Christians. In 3:17-18 their self-satisfaction is criticized in terms of the city's major industries. Although they imagine themselves to be rich and self-sufficient, they are in fact poor (despite the banking industry), blind (despite the medical school and its eye-salves), and naked (despite the manufacture of clothes and blankets there). However, the risen Christ offers to them genuine spiritual riches: the well-tested gold (through suffering) that brings true wealth, the white garment promised to the victor who has remained a faithful witness (see 3:5), and effective eye-salve that makes spiritual sight possible. In 3:19b they are urged to be more zealous and to repent of their spiritual lukewarmness. Evoking the figure of the lover in Canticles 5:2 ("Behold, I stand at the door and knock"), the risen Christ in 3:20 promises to share his meal (the Messiah's banquet) with those who respond positively to him (see Jn 10:3; 16:23; 18:37).

The "victor" saying in 3:21 promises those who remain faithful in their witness a share in the glory of the risen Christ. Just as Christ in his death and resurrection won the victory over death and Satan, and so was granted the privilege of sharing God's throne (see Rv 21:2; 22:3; Col 3:1), so also his faithful witnesses will share the same throne (see Rv 20:4; Mt 19:28; Lk 22:30; 2 Tm 2:11-12). The final call to hear (3:22) follows the usual pattern.

For Reflection: Many "First World" Christians in the United States and Europe find themselves (and their cultures) in a state of apparent self-sufficiency and self-satisfaction that is analogous to that of the Laodicean Christians. Relying on their wealth, material prosperity, and technical knowledge, they find it hard to recognize their own neediness and spiritual blindness. Do you find signs of this phenomenon in your church? What are they? How can they be remedied?

IV

The Heavenly Court, the Scroll
and the Lamb

The vision of the heavenly court, the scroll and the Lamb is a good example of the nature of Revelation as a whole. The motif of the heavenly court, with the supreme God presiding over the divine council, is very ancient and well represented in ancient Near Eastern and biblical literatures. The specific features of the heavenly court as they are described in Revelation 4–5 are taken from various biblical texts: Ezekiel 1 and 10, Isaiah 6, Exodus 19, and Daniel 7. Yet there are no direct quotations, and there are many changes and new combinations. For John the seer, as for other Jewish writers of the time, creativity consisted not in manufacturing the utterly "new" but rather in using the "old" in new combinations. Almost every phrase in Revelation 4–5 is old, but the picture of the heavenly court is new and distinctively Christian.

The vision of God and the Lamb presiding over the heavenly throne room also sent a political message. If God the Father of Jesus Christ the Lamb is Lord of all, then the Roman emperor is not. That John or any of his readers had ever seen the imperial throne room is highly unlikely. Nevertheless, they could imagine what it was like. Thus the vision of the heavenly throne room served to relativize the claims of every earthly ruler, including the emperor.

The Heavenly Court (4:1-11)

[1] After this I had a vision of an open door to heaven, and I heard the trumpet-like voice that had spoken to me before, saying, "Come up here and I will show you what must happen afterwards." [2] At once I was caught up in spirit. A throne was there in heaven, and on the throne sat [3] one whose appearance sparkled like jasper and carnelian. Around the throne was a halo as brilliant as an emerald. [4] Surrounding the throne I saw twenty-four other thrones on which twenty-four elders sat, dressed in white garments and with gold crowns on their heads. [5] From the throne came flashes of lightning, rumblings, and peals of thunder. Seven flaming torches burned in front of the throne, which are the seven spirits of God. [6] In front of the throne was something that resembled a sea of glass like crystal.

In the center and around the throne, there were four living creatures covered with eyes in front and in back. [7] The first creature resembled a lion, the second was like a calf, the third had a face like that of a human being, and the fourth looked like an eagle in flight. [8] The four living creatures, each of them with six wings, were covered with eyes inside and out. Day and night they do not stop exclaiming:

"Holy, holy, holy is the Lord God almighty,
who was, and who is, and who is to come."

[9] Whenever the living creatures give glory and honor and thanks to the one who sits on the throne, who lives forever and ever, [10] the twenty-four elders fall down before the one who sits on the throne and worship him, who lives forever and ever. They throw down their crowns before the throne, exclaiming:

[11] "Worthy are you,
Lord our God, to receive glory and honor and power,
for you created all things;

because of your will they came to be and were created."

After the invitation to John to come up to the heavenly court (4:1-2a), there are descriptions of the throne and of the one seated on it (4:2b-3), of the twenty-four elders (4:4), of the throne and related phenomena (4:5-6a), of the four living creatures (4:6b-8), and of the worship of God by the living creatures and by the elders (4:9-11).

In 4:1-2a the seer is invited to a vision of the heavenly court. The invitation takes the form of "an open door to heaven" and a trumpet-like voice (see 1:10). The experience of the seer is ecstatic ("caught up in spirit," see 1:10), and is like that of the prophet Ezekiel: "the heavens opened, and I saw divine visions" (Ez 1:1). The content of the vision is "what must happen afterwards"—which refers not so much to what happens in chapter 4 as to what is described thereafter.

What first catches the seer's eye (4:2b-3) is the heavenly throne and the one seated upon it. God is obviously the occupant of the throne. But the description of God avoids human features (anthropomorphism), and instead uses comparisons with various gems (as in Ex 28:17-21)—jasper, carnelian, emerald—to express the dazzling brilliance of the one seated on God's throne (see Ez 1:26-28).

The description of the twenty-four thrones and the twenty-four elders in 4:4 makes these figures clearly subordinate to God. Neither gods nor even angels, the elders seem to represent the people of God (the twelve tribes and/or apostles times two). And so they wear the white garments of victory and bear the golden crowns of those who have already been granted the victory.

The second description of the heavenly throne in 4:5-6a adds to the mood of brilliance with three sets of biblical images. The "flashes of lightning, rumblings, and peals of thunder" evoke the experience of ancient Israel at Mount Sinai (see Ex 19:16). The "seven flaming torches" evoke the prophet Zechariah's vision of the lampstand with seven torches (see Zec 4:2; Rv 1:12), and the reference to the seven spirits of God is already familiar from Revelation 1:4, 20. The glassy sea-like crystal evokes Ezekiel's inaugural vision (see Ez 1:22) and perhaps alludes to the ancient motif of God's victory in creation over the sea as the symbol of chaos. Now the sea is brilliant and placid, fully under God's orderly control.

The description of the four living creatures (4:6b-8) in the heavenly throne room combines material from Ezekiel 1 and Isaiah 6. The list of animals to which they are compared in 4:7—lion, calf, human being, and eagle—appears also in Ezekiel 1:10. (In the second century these four figures were equated with the four Evangelists, but that symbolism should not be read into this text.) That the creatures are "covered with eyes" (4:6b, 8) indicates that they see everything around them. Their wings (4:8; see Ez 1:6, 8) suggest an identification with the Cherubim depicted in the Jerusalem Temple (see Ez 10). Their "six wings" moves the description in the direction of Isaiah 6 (see 6:2) and prepares for their song, "Holy, holy, holy is the Lord God almighty," which is based on Isaiah 6:3. The second part of their hymn ("who was, and who is, and who is to come") uses the divine title previously found in 1:4.

61

The worship accorded to God by the four living creatures and the twenty-four elders (4:9-11) focuses on God's creative power and on his identity as the "Lord our God"—despite the Roman emperor's pretentions to be Lord and God. There seems to be a coordination between the worship offered by the four living creatures (4:9) and that offered by the twenty-four elders (4:10). Throwing their crowns (see 4:4) before God's throne is a sign of the elders' submission and obeisance (4:10b). Whereas the praise from the four living creatures (4:8b) focuses on the essential nature of God ("Holy, holy, holy . . . who was, and who is, and who is to come"), the praise from the elders (4:11) emphasizes God's glory shown forth in creation. The expression "worthy . . . to receive" prepares for the formula applied to the Lamb in 5:9, 12. The emphasis in 4:11b is on God's sovereign will in creating all things. In the background may be attempts to apply the Latin titles *dominus et Deus* ("lord and god") to the emperor Domitian.

For Reflection: Imagine yourself as John the seer invited to a vision of the heavenly court. Spend some time contemplating the various elements of the vision. What do you see? What do you hear? How do you feel as a result? Can you make your own the praises given to God by the heavenly creatures (see 4:8b, 11)?

The Scroll and the Lamb (5:1-14)

[1] I saw a scroll in the right hand of the one who sat on the throne. It had writing on both sides and was sealed with seven seals. [2] Then I saw a mighty angel who proclaimed in a loud voice, "Who is worthy to open the scroll and break its seals?" [3] But no one in heaven or on

earth or under the earth was able to open the scroll or to examine it. ⁴ I shed many tears because no one was found worthy to open the scroll or to examine it. ⁵ One of the elders said to me, "Do not weep. The lion of the tribe of Judah, the root of David, has triumphed, enabling him to open the scroll with its seven seals."

⁶ Then I saw standing in the midst of the throne and the four living creatures and the elders a Lamb that seemed to have been slain. He has seven horns and seven eyes; these are the [seven] spirits of God sent out into the whole world. ⁷ He came and received the scroll from the right hand of the one who sat on the throne. ⁸ When he took it, the four living creatures and the twenty-four elders fell down before the Lamb. Each of the elders held a harp and gold bowls filled with incense, which are the prayers of the holy ones. ⁹ They sang a new hymn:

"Worthy are you to receive the scroll
    and to break open its seals,
    for you were slain and with your blood you purchased for God
    those from every tribe and tongue,
    people and nation.
¹⁰ You made them a kingdom and priests for our God,
    and they will reign on earth."

¹¹ I looked again and heard the voice of many angels who surrounded the throne and the living creatures and the elders. They were countless in number, and ¹² they cried out in a loud voice:

"Worthy is the Lamb that was slain
    to receive power and riches, wisdom and strength,
    honor and glory and blessing."

¹³ Then I heard every creature in heaven and on earth and under the earth and in the sea, everything in the universe, cry out:

"To the one who sits on the throne and to the Lamb
   be blessing and honor, glory and might,
   forever and ever."
¹⁴ The four living creatures answered, "Amen," and
the elders fell down and worshiped.

The action in the heavenly court moves forward with
the search for someone worthy to open the scroll with
seven seals (5:1-5). The slain Lamb (Jesus Christ, who
died and was raised) emerges as the only one worthy to do
so (5:6-7). He is celebrated in turn by the four living creatures and the twenty-four elders (5:8-10), the angels
(5:11-12), and all creation (5:13), along with an "Amen"
from the four living creatures and more homage from the
twenty-four elders (5:14).

In 5:1 John sees a book in the form of a roll or scroll on
God's hand (a surprising anthropomorphism in view of
4:3 where God's physical features are avoided). That the
scroll had writing on both sides suggests a surplus of content, and that it was sealed with seven seals indicates that
it is "top secret." The content of the scroll is presumably
"what must happen afterwards" (see 4:2). The challenge
to find someone worthy to open the seals (see 5:2-3) is
broadcast over all creation ("in heaven or on earth or under the earth"). The "worthy" one must possess the appropriate moral stature; it is not simply a matter of physical
strength. He will open the scroll by breaking its seals. According to 5:4, the seer weeps because no one is found
worthy, and so the revelation and its actual unfolding will
be withheld. But in 5:5 he is reassured by one of the elders
that one has been found worthy to open the scroll. He is
Jesus Christ—"the lion of the tribe of Judah" (see Gn
49:9) and "the root of David" (see Is 11:1, 10). Through

his death and resurrection, Jesus has triumphed (see 3:21) and so he alone can open the scroll.

In 5:6-7 the slain and risen Christ comes forward and takes hold of the scroll. John sees him apparently standing between God's throne and the four living creatures and twenty-four elders. He sees him as "a Lamb that seemed to have been slain"—surely a reference to Jesus as the Suffering Servant of God (see Is 53:7, "like a lamb led to the slaughter"). The risen Jesus "seemed to have been slain" in the sense that he bore the marks of his suffering (see Jn 20:24-29), even though he is now a glorious figure. His "seven horns" allude to his perfect strength, and his "seven eyes" refer to his perfect knowledge. For the "seven spirits" see 1:4; 3:1; and 4:5. As in Zechariah 4:10, the spirits are sent to spy out the earth. Only the slain and risen Christ has been found worthy to receive the scroll from God's right hand. By his death and resurrection, Jesus has already inaugurated the sequence of events to come ("what must happen afterwards"), and so it is fitting that he should be the one to reveal what still must unfold.

The slain Lamb found worthy to open the scroll is celebrated first by the four living creatures and the twenty-four elders (5:8-10). They all prostrate themselves before him to do him homage. With their harps and incense bowls the elders ready themselves for prayer. The parenthetical identification of the incense bowls as the "prayers of the holy ones" (Christians) in 5:8 is based on Psalm 141:2: "Let my prayer come like incense before you." The "new hymn" refers to the new thing done by God in and through the slain Lamb—which in turn deserves a new song (see Pss 33:3; 40:4; 96:1; 98:1; 144:9; 149:1). The song in 5:9-10 focuses on the saving effects of

Jesus' death ("you were slain") in terms of universal redemption ("you were purchased by God") and the royal priesthood ("a kingdom and priests for our God"). Through Christ every Christian is a king and a priest (see 1:6; 20:6; Ex 19:6; Is 61:6), and will share in Christ's reign on earth (see chap. 20). The persecuted Christians, not the emperors and their officials, constitute the true kings of the earth.

The second round of praise (5:11-12) comes from the angels on the outside circles of the heavenly throne room. Their praise focuses on the moral stature of the slain Lamb ("worthy is the Lamb"). The first four members in the list ("power and wisdom, riches and strength") concern the qualities of the Lamb, and the final three ("honor and glory and blessing") refer to what others must do in response to him.

The third round of praise (5:13) involves all created beings—the whole universe. Their praise is directed jointly to God and to Christ ("To the one who sits on the throne and to the Lamb"), thus suggesting a high view of Christ as equal with God. Recall Pliny the Elder's comment that the early Christians (from roughly the same time and place as those addressed in Revelation) sang hymns to Christ "as to a god" (*Epistles* 10.96). The four members of this list ("blessing and honor, glory and might") express the proper response of all creation to the Lamb and to God. The prayers of praise are sealed in 5:14 by the "Amen" from the four living creatures and by the prostration of the twenty-four elders.

For Reflection: The richness of the sights and sounds in this text should not obscure the theological claims made here. The only one worthy to open the scroll that describes the future triumph of God is "the Lamb that was slain"—the crucified Jesus of Nazareth. Through his death and resurrection the victory has been won. Those who are faithful to him already share his redemptive action and enjoy the dignity of his royal priesthood. So great is the dignity of the Lamb that he can be placed on the same level as God. How does contemplation of this scene contribute to your appreciation of the crucified and risen Christ and his significance in your life?

V

The Seven Seals

Taking as its starting point the seven seals on the scroll, the first sequence of future events concerns war (6:1-2), strife among nations (6:3-4), famine (6:5-6), death (6:7-8), persecution (6:9-11), the great tribulation (6:12-17), and silence (8:1). Between the sixth and seventh seals there is an interlude that depicts the faithful witnesses who are sealed before the great tribulation (7:1-8) and who have suffered martyrdom and already share the glory of the Lamb (7:9-17). There are close parallels between this sequence of future events and those mentioned in the "little apocalpyse" of the Synoptic Gospels (see Mk 13, Mt 24, and Lk 21).

The First Six Seals (6:1-17)

¹ Then I watched while the Lamb broke open the first of the seven seals, and I heard one of the four living creatures cry out in a voice like thunder, "Come forward." ² I looked, and there was a white horse, and its rider had a bow. He was given a crown, and he rode forth victorious to further his victories.

³ When he broke open the second seal, I heard the second living creature cry out, "Come forward." ⁴ Another horse came out, a red one. Its rider was given power to take peace away from the earth, so that people

would slaughter one another. And he was given a huge sword.

⁵ When he broke open the third seal, I heard the third living creature cry out, "Come forward." I looked, and there was a black horse, and its rider held a scale in his hand. ⁶ I heard what seemed to be a voice in the midst of the four living creatures. It said, "A ration of wheat costs a day's pay, and three rations of barley cost a day's pay. But do not damage the olive oil or the wine."

⁷ When he broke open the fourth seal, I heard the voice of the fourth living creature cry out, "Come forward." ⁸ I looked, and there was a pale green horse. Its rider was named Death, and Hades accompanied him. They were given authority over a quarter of the earth, to kill with sword, famine, and plague, and by means of the beasts of the earth.

⁹ When he broke open the fifth seal, I saw underneath the altar the souls of those who had been slaughtered because of the witness they bore to the word of God. ¹⁰ They cried out in a loud voice, "How long will it be, holy and true master, before you sit in judgment and avenge our blood on the inhabitants of the earth?" ¹¹ Each of them was given a white robe, and they were told to be patient a little while longer until the number was filled of their fellow servants and brothers who were going to be killed as they had been.

¹² Then I watched while he broke open the sixth seal, and there was a great earthquake; the sun turned as black as dark sackcloth and the whole moon became like blood. ¹³ The stars in the sky fell to the earth like unripe figs shaken loose from the tree in a strong wind. ¹⁴ Then the sky was divided like a torn scroll curling up, and every mountain and island was moved from its place. ¹⁵ The kings of the earth, the nobles, the military officers, the rich, the powerful, and every slave and free person hid themselves in caves and among mountain crags. ¹⁶ They cried out to the mountains and the rocks,

"Fall on us and hide us from the face of the one who sits on the throne and from the wrath of the Lamb, [17] because the great day of their wrath has come and who can withstand it?"

The descriptions of the opening of the first four seals (6:1-8) follow the same basic literary pattern. The Lamb (the risen Christ) opens the seal; one of the four living creatures says, "Come forward"; and John sees a colored horse with its rider. The motif of the colored horses echoes texts in Zechariah (see 1:8-10; 6:1-8), though as is customary in Revelation there are differences.

The opening of the first seal (6:1-2) reveals a white horse and a rider with a bow. The bow was the characteristic weapon of the Parthians (ancient Persians), the enemy that Rome feared most. The "crown" and the mentions of victory probably evoked popular (at least among subject peoples) predictions that the Parthians would eventually defeat the Romans in war.

The opening of the second seal (6:3-4) reveals a red horse and a rider with a huge sword. This rider is allowed to take away the (false) peace that existed among the nations within the Roman empire and to foment international strife.

The opening of the third seal (6:5-6) reveals a black horse and a rider with a scale, which is needed for weighing food during famine. Because food is in short supply, it must be weighed and sold (at exorbitant prices). To pay a denarius (a whole day's wage according to Matthew 20:2) for a daily supply of food indicates how desperate conditions will be. There may be an allusion to an actual famine that occurred around A.D. 92 during the reign of the emperor Domitian. The closing directive ("but do not damage the olive oil or the wine") remains mysterious. Are these luxury goods that foolish people still demand in the midst of famine? Or are these goods exempted from the rationing? Is there a reference to Domitian's prohibition in A.D. 92 against planting more vineyards?

The opening of the fourth seal (6:7-8) reveals a pale green horse and Death as its rider, with Hades (the abode of the dead) as his companion. The death brought by Death will take many forms ("sword, famine and plague, and by means of the beasts of the earth"), though there are limits placed on his power ("over a quarter of the earth").

The opening of the first four seals—war, strife among nations, famine, and death—will interrupt the smooth running of the Roman empire and throw it into chaos. These plagues are personified by the various riders. There may be some relation between the plagues and the colors of the horses: white (victory in battle), red (bloodshed), black (famine), and pale green (death).

The opening of the fifth seal (6:9-11) concerns the Christian martyrs and the persecutions that result in their martyrdoms. In 6:9 John sees an altar in heaven. The biblical background of the heavenly altar is the earthly altar of holocausts described in Leviticus 4:7 at the base of which the blood of sacrificial animals was poured out. Since "life" was understood to be in the blood (see Lv 17:11), one could say that the "souls" of these sacrificial animals were underneath the altar. The application of this imagery to the Christian martyrs indicates that their death was interpreted as a sacrifice offered to God. The reason for their martyrdom was the faithful "witness they bore to the word of God"—to the gospel. These martyrdoms had already occurred, most likely under the emperor Nero in the early sixties of the first century A.D.

In 6:10 the martyrs ask God ("the holy and true master") how long it will be before God will preside at the last judgment and will punish the wicked perpetrators of the persecution. Note that vengeance remains a divine prerogative (see Dt 32:35; Rom 12:19), not something to be undertaken by humans. The victorious martyrs are given white robes as a symbol of their victory (see 6:11). They are told to be patient, because the last judgment will not come until another round of persecutions takes place under Domitian in the nineties of the first century A.D. Unlike the Synoptic "little apocalypse" where persecutions and martyrdoms are presented as being wholly future (see Mk 13:9-13; Mt 10:17-22; Lk 21:12-17), in Revelation some martyrdoms had already occurred under Nero (notably those of Peter and Paul) and still more are anticipated under Domitian. The idea underlying 6:11 seems to be that of a fixed number or quota of martyrs to be reached before the end can come (see the Jewish apocalypse 4 Ezra 4:35-36 for the same concept). Paul in Romans 11:25-26 makes a similar point when he speaks about "the full number of Gentiles" coming in before "all Israel" can be saved.

The opening of the sixth seal (6:12-17) involves cosmic events that are associated in the Synoptic apocalypses with the "great tribulation" (see Mk 13:24-25; Mt 24:29; Lk 21:25-26). The passage first lists the cosmic signs (6:12-14) and then considers their impact on human beings (6:15-17). The language used in connection with the cosmic signs is based largely on various Old Testament passages: the earthquake (Am 8:8; 9:5), the moon (Jl

2:31), the stars and the sky (Is 34:4), and so forth. The images are striking: dark sackcloth—a sign of mourning (the sun), unripe figs shaken from a tree (the stars), and a torn scroll curling up (the sky). The human beings who react to these cosmic signs fall into seven categories, ranging from kings to slaves (6:15). Their plea to be hidden away by mountains and rocks is based on Hosea 10:8 (see Lk 23:30). What they fear is the definitive judgment by God and the Lamb. By their fear they acknowledge their own guilt and the sovereignty of God and of the Lamb. The divine judgment constitutes the climax of the scenario of the opening of the first six seals.

For Reflection: The visions associated with the first six seals helped the people of John's communities to put their present (innocent) sufferings into the wider context of God's plan. The assumption is that God as sovereign Lord will vindicate those who suffer for the sake of the gospel—just as God has already vindicated Jesus in his resurrection and exaltation. And so there is great confidence in the ultimate victory of God and the Lamb, and hope that the faithful witnesses will share their victory fully. In reflecting on the opening of the first six seals, one can and should exercise imagination to enter the visions of John by trying to see what he saw and to hear what he heard. And yet it is also important to bear in mind the fundamental theological truths behind these visions: the sovereignty of God, the pivotal significance of the slain Lamb (who is the risen Christ), and trust that God will vindicate the righteous and punish the wicked (the justice of God). How do the visions associated with the opening of the six seals express these truths?

The Sealing of the 144,000 (7:1-17), and the Seventh Seal (8:1)

[1] After this I saw four angels standing at the four corners of the earth, holding back the four winds of the earth so that no wind could blow on land or sea or against any tree. [2] Then I saw another angel come up from the East, holding the seal of the living God. He cried out in a loud voice to the four angels who were given power to damage the land and the sea, [3] "Do not damage the land or the sea or the trees until we put the seal on the foreheads of the servants of our God."

[4] I heard the number of those who had been marked with the seal, one hundred and forty-four thousand marked from every tribe of the Israelites: [5] twelve thousand were marked from the tribe of Judah, twelve thousand from the tribe of Reuben, twelve thousand from the tribe of Gad, [6] twelve thousand from the tribe of Asher, twelve thousand from the tribe of Naphtali, twelve thousand from the tribe of Manasseh, [7] twelve thousand from the tribe of Simeon, twelve thousand from the tribe of Levi, twelve thousand from the tribe of Issachar, [8] twelve thousand from the tribe of Zebulun, twelve thousand from the tribe of Joseph, and twelve thousand were marked from the tribe of Benjamin.

[9] After this I had a vision of a great multitude, which no one could count, from every nation, race, people, and tongue. They stood before the throne and before the Lamb, wearing white robes and holding palm branches in their hands. [10] They cried out in a loud voice:

"Salvation comes from our God, who is seated on the throne,
and from the Lamb."

[11] All the angels stood around the throne and around the elders and the four living creatures. They prostrated

themselves before the throne, worshiped God, [12] and exclaimed:

"Amen. Blessing and glory, wisdom and
thanksgiving,
honor, power, and might
be to our God forever and ever. Amen."

[13] Then one of the elders spoke up and said to me, "Who are these wearing white robes, and where did they come from?" [14] I said to him, "My lord, you are the one who knows." He said to me, "These are the ones who have survived the time of great distress; they have washed their robes and made them white in the blood of the Lamb.

[15] For this reason they stand before God's throne
and worship him day and night in his temple.
The one who sits on the throne will shelter them.
[16] They will not hunger or thirst anymore,
nor will the sun or any heat strike them.
[17] For the Lamb who is in the center of the throne
will shepherd them
and lead them to springs of life-giving water,
and God will wipe away every tear from their eyes."

[8:1] When he broke open the seventh seal, there was silence in heaven for about half an hour.

As is the case with other series of sevens in Revelation, there is an interlude between the sixth and seventh items. The break makes it possible for the 144,000 to be sealed (7:1-8) and for the triumph of the elect ones to be celebrated (7:9-17). The opening of the seventh seal is narrated in 8:1.

The beginning of the interlude (7:1) assumes that the earth is a square or a cube, and that four angels have control over its four corners. Their holding back the winds of destruction—probably associated with the cosmic upheavals described in 6:12-14—makes the interlude possible. In 7:2-3 the other angel from the East holds the "seal" of the living God and orders the four angels to hold off until the servants of God have been sealed. The idea of the seal here implies divine possession and protection (see Ez 9:4-7). In the context of Revelation the seal will protect the faithful against the forces of Satan during the "great tribulation." The concept is similar to the final petition in the Lord's Prayer: "And do not subject us to the final test, but deliver us from the evil one" (Mt 6:13).

The number of those who are sealed in 7:4-8 is 144,000, which is twelve times twelve times one thousand. The prominence of the number twelve and its multiple is obviously related to the twelve tribes of Israel as constituting the full people of God. Those who are sealed, however, are not exclusively Jews or Jewish Christians. Rather, these persons represent the whole people of God. The point is not the exact number but what that number represents. The list in 7:5-8 has some peculiar features. The order of the tribes follows no obvious historical or logical sequence. Judah comes first—presumably because Jesus the Messiah came from Judah. Dan is omitted—perhaps because of its association with idolatry and the antichrist. Manasseh, the son of Joseph, takes the place of Dan.

The second scene in the interlude (7:9-17) concerns the "great multitude" of martyrs (7:9). They already enjoy access to the heavenly throne and the Lamb. Their victory is symbolized by their white robes and palm branches (see 1 Mc 13:51; 2 Mc 10:7). Their song in 7:10 acknowledges that they owe their "salvation" to God and the Lamb, no matter how heroic they have been. Note that "salvation" here refers to eternal life with God, and that God and the Lamb are placed on the same level.

In 7:11-12 the angels affirm the martyrs' triumph. One gets the impression of circles expanding outward from the heavenly throne: the four living creatures, the elders, the angels, and (perhaps on the outer circle) the martyrs. The angels' song also attributes the martyrs' salvation to God. Their song begins and ends with "Amen" (I believe! or Yes!), and ascribes to God seven qualities or attributes ("Blessing . . . might").

The precise identity of the great multitude is made clear from the dialogue in 7:13-14 between the elder and the seer. The elder first inquires from John about who these people are. John in turn asks the elder for enlightenment. The elder then describes them as "the ones who have survived the time of great distress." Thus the interlude rejoins the series of the seven seals, for the sixth seal includes the "great tribulation." We are apparently to imagine that even during the tribulation the martyrdoms continue. The theology of martyrdom is expressed (paradoxically) in 7:14c: "they have washed their robes and made them white in the blood of the Lamb." Their white robes are a sign of victory, and the source of their victory is the death of Jesus ("the blood of the Lamb"). Through his blood their robes have been washed and made white.

The heavenly happiness that the martyrs experience is described in 7:15-17. On the one hand (7:15), their blessed life consists in enjoying God's presence and worshiping God. The "temple" is not on earth (in Jerusalem) but rather in the heavenly throne room, where God makes his dwelling and "shelters" those who belong to God. On the other hand (7:16-17), the victorious martyrs are freed from the sufferings associated with human existence (hunger, thirst, etc.). The language of 7:16-17b is taken from Isaiah 49:10, and that of 7:17c from Isaiah 25:8. At the center of the scene, however, is the Lamb—a figure not found in the Isaiah texts but the christological center of the elder's description of the martyrs' bliss. Again God and the Lamb are placed on the same level of importance.

The opening of the seventh seal (8:1) issues in "silence in heaven for about half an hour." The precise meaning is elusive. It could be that the heavenly choruses cease singing so that the prayers of the saints on earth might be heard. Or (more likely) it could be that the perfection of the heavenly worship ultimately transcends speech and song, and so silence is the appropriate praise for God in the fullness of the kingdom.

For Reflection: The interlude highlights God's protection for his people and the victory already shared by the martyrs. It presupposes the experience of persecution and martyrdom under the emperor Nero (when Peter and Paul are believed to have been killed). John expects further instances of martyrdom under the emperor Domitian. The martyrs imitate the example of the "slain Lamb" and share in his triumph. Their triumph has been made possible "by the blood of the Lamb." Martyrdom is not confined to the first Christian centuries or to the Roman empire. Can you name some recent martyrs? What constitutes martyrdom? On the basis of Revelation can you discern the outlines of a theology of martyrdom?

VI

The First Six Trumpets

The series of the seven trumpets extends from 8:2 to 11:19. After a transitional passage about the angels and the golden censer (8:2-6), there are four short descriptions of punishments cast upon the earth (8:7, 8-9, 10-11, 12-13) and two longer ones (9:1-12, 13-19)—all signaled by the blast of a trumpet. The concluding comment in 9:20-21 provides the key to understanding these punish ments: They are intended to lead evildoers away from their idolatry and related sins. The two scenes in the interlude (10:1-11; 11:1-14) as well as the seventh trumpet (11:15-19) conclude the second sequence. They will be treated in the next chapter.

The First Six Trumpets (8:2–9:21)

² And I saw that the seven angels who stood before God were given seven trumpets.

³ Another angel came and stood at the altar, holding a gold censer. He was given a great quantity of incense to offer, along with the prayers of all the holy ones, on the gold altar that was before the throne. ⁴ The smoke of the incense along with the prayers of the holy ones went up before God from the hand of the angel. ⁵ Then the angel took the censer, filled it with burning coals from the al- tar, and hurled it down to the earth. There were peals of

thunder, rumblings, flashes of lightning, and an earthquake.

⁶ The seven angels who were holding the seven trumpets prepared to blow them.

⁷ When the first one blew his trumpet, there came hail and fire mixed with blood, which was hurled down to the earth. A third of the land was burned up, along with a third of the trees and all green grass.

⁸ When the second angel blew his trumpet, something like a large burning mountain was hurled into the sea. A third of the sea turned to blood, ⁹ a third of the creatures living in the sea died, and a third of the ships were wrecked.

¹⁰ When the third angel blew his trumpet, a large star burning like a torch fell from the sky. It fell on a third of the rivers and on the springs of water. ¹¹ The star was called "Wormwood," and a third of all the water turned to wormwood. Many people died from this water, because it was made bitter.

¹² When the fourth angel blew his trumpet, a third of the sun, a third of the moon, and a third of the stars were struck, so that a third of them became dark. The day lost its light for a third of the time, as did the night.

¹³ Then I looked again and heard an eagle flying high overhead cry out in a loud voice, "Woe! Woe! Woe to the inhabitants of the earth from the rest of the trumpet blasts that the three angels are about to blow!"

⁹:¹ Then the fifth angel blew his trumpet, and I saw a star that had fallen from the sky to the earth. It was given the key for the passage to the abyss. ² It opened the passage to the abyss and smoke came up out of the passage like smoke from a huge furnace. The sun and the air were darkened by the smoke from the passage.

³ Locusts came out of the smoke onto the land, and they were given the same power as scorpions of the earth. ⁴ They were told not to harm the grass of the earth or any plant or any tree, but only those people who did

not have the seal of God on their foreheads. [5] They were not allowed to kill them but only to torment them for five months; the torment they inflicted was like that of a scorpion when it stings a person. [6] During that time these people will seek death but will not find it, and they will long to die but death will escape them.

[7] The appearance of the locusts was like that of horses ready for battle. On their heads they wore what looked like crowns of gold; their faces were like human faces, [8] and they had hair like women's hair. Their teeth were like lions' teeth, and [9] they had chests like iron breastplates. The sound of their wings was like the sound of many horse-drawn chariots racing into battle. [10] They had tails like scorpions, with stingers; with their tails they had power to harm people for five months. [11] They had as their king the angel of the abyss, whose name in Hebrew is Abaddon and in Greek Apollyon.

[12] The first woe has passed, but there are two more to come.

[13] Then the sixth angel blew his trumpet, and I heard a voice coming from the [four] horns of the gold altar before God, [14] telling the sixth angel who held the trumpet, "Release the four angels who are bound at the banks of the great river Euphrates." [15] So the four angels were released, who were prepared for this hour, day, month, and year to kill a third of the human race. [16] The number of cavalry troops was two hundred million; I heard their number. [17] Now in my vision this is how I saw the horses and their riders. They wore red, blue, and yellow breastplates, and the horses' heads were like heads of lions, and out of their mouths came fire, smoke, and sulfur. [18] By these three plagues of fire, smoke, and sulfur that came out of their mouths a third of the human race was killed. [19] For the powers of horses is in their mouths and in their tails; for their tails are like snakes, with heads that inflict harm.

[20] The rest of the human race, who were not killed by these plagues, did not repent of the works of their hands, to give up the worship of demons and idols made from gold, silver, bronze, stone, and wood, which cannot see or hear or walk. [21] Nor did they repent of their murders, their magic potions, their unchastity, or their robberies.

The opening of the seven seals means that the scroll itself is open and presumably what follows represents the content of the scroll. The description of the angels and the censer in 8:2-6 serves as a bridge between the seven seals and the seven trumpets. The "seven angels" (8:2) are apparently the seven archangels or the "angels of the presence" (see Is 63:9; Tb 12:15) who minister to God at the heavenly throne. They will blow seven trumpets in turn. In the meantime (8:3-5), another angel holds a golden censer and places in it a large amount of incense. The censer first (8:3b-4; see Ps 141:2) serves as the vehicle to bring up to God the prayers of the saints on earth. The imagery evokes the description of the altar of incense in Exodus 30. But here, of course, the altar is in heaven. The holy ones on earth are making the prayer attributed to the martyrs in 6:10: "How long will it be, holy and true master, before you sit in judgment and avenge our blood on the inhabitants of the earth?" Then in 8:5 the censer serves as a prelude to the various punishments hurled down upon the earth in the effort to make sinners see the error of their ways. Cosmic signs accompany the angel's action. All this is in preparation for the seven angels to blow their trumpets and bring down the punishments (8:6).

The descriptions of the first four trumpets (8:7-13) are similar in form and size. Their content evokes motifs from the book of Exodus, and in most cases "a third" of something is harmed. For the association between the trumpet and the Day of the Lord, see Joel 2:1; Isaiah 27:13; Zechariah 9:14; and Zephaniah 1:16.

When the first trumpet is sounded (8:7), hail and fire mixed with blood (see Ex 9:24; Jl 3:3) come upon the earth and burn up a third of the land and the trees and "all green grass" (but see 9:4, where the locusts are told not to harm the grass).

When the second trumpet is sounded (8:8-9), a large burning mountain is cast into the sea and turns a third of the sea into blood (see Ex 7:20), kills a third of the sea creatures, and wrecks a third of the ships.

When the third trumpet is sounded (8:10-11), a large star burning like a torch falls upon a third of the rivers and springs, and makes their water bitter (see Ex 15:23). The star is named "Wormwood" after a bitter and harmful plant. The prophet Jeremiah referred to it when he described God punishing the people's sins (see Jer 9:14; 23:15).

When the fourth trumpet is sounded (8:12), there is darkness in a third of the sun, moon, and stars. The result is darkness upon the earth (see Ex 10:21; Am 8:9). In 8:13 an eagle serves as God's messenger. With a triple "Woe!" (see 9:12; 11:14), he warns of worse punishments to come.

The descriptions of the plagues associated with the fifth trumpet (9:1-12) and the sixth trumpet (9:13-19) are more detailed and even more terrifying. When the fifth trumpet is sounded, a star falls to earth and opens the shaft connecting the earth to the underworld (9:1-2). The star is personified; perhaps an angel is to be understood.

The "abyss" is the abode of Satan and the fallen angels (see 20:7-10). The idea is rooted in the biblical concept of Sheol as the abode of the dead and in the Greek idea of Hades. By opening the shaft, the star/angel lets loose the smoke from the abyss and so darkens the sun and the air.

Out of the smoke comes the plague of locusts (9:3-6). These locusts, however, are commissioned not to harm the foliage (their usual food) but rather to torment with a sting like that of scorpions those who still refuse to worship God and the Lamb—those "who did not have the seal of God on their foreheads" (see 7:1-8). Again the motive behind the punishments seems to be to shock evildoers into recognizing their sinfulness and to have them reform their lives (see 9:20-21). The punishments, however excruciating they may be, do not end in death and are of limited duration ("five months").

The description of the locusts in 9:7-10 adds to the terror. These are no ordinary locusts. By a series of eight comparisons ("the appearance . . . was like") one gets not a clear picture but rather a series of incompatible features from animals, humans, and even metal that serve to form a monster. In 9:11 the leader of the locusts is identified as the "angel of the abyss." His name in Hebrew ("Abaddon") means "destruction" and in Greek ("Apollyon"—perhaps a pun on the Greek god Apollo) means "destroyer." In 9:12 the fifth trumpet is equated with the first "woe" (see 8:13), with still two more to come.

When the sixth trumpet is sounded (9:13), John tells first what he heard (9:14) and its projected result (9:15-16), and then what he saw (9:17) and its projected result (9:18-19). John heard the voice from the heavenly

84

altar ordering the release of the four angels bound at the banks of the Euphrates River. This was the river that the Parthians (Persians) needed to cross to begin their offensive against the Roman armies. Their huge army of two-hundred million cavalry troops would be given permission to kill a third of the human race.

John saw the horses and their riders. More destructive than the riders are the horses whose "heads were like heads of lions, and out of their mouths came fire, smoke, and sulfur" (9:17). The latter three items are the means by which a third of the human race is to be killed (9:18). The sixth trumpet ends with parenthetical (and curious) remarks about the relative power of the horses' heads and tails.

The concluding comment in 9:20-21 suggests that the purpose of the punishments—to bring about repentance among sinful humankind—will not be achieved. Instead, humans will continue in their idolatrous ways—worshiping demons (false gods) and graven images. For idolatry as the root sin and the source of all other sins, see Paul's meditation on Gentile humankind before and apart from Christ in Romans 1:18-32. And so the list of sins in 9:21—murders, magic potions (including abortifacients?), unchastity, and robbery—is what can be expected from those who fail to recognize the sovereignty of God and the Lamb.

For Reflection: The first four trumpets signal disasters that will affect large parts of the land and sea and even the earth's sources of light. The fifth trumpet signals a plague of locusts that will inflict pain on humans, and the sixth trumpet portrays a huge army that will kill a third of the human race. The purpose of these punishments is apparently to shock sinful humankind into acknowledging the sovereignty of God. There is ample material here on which one can profitably exercise the senses and the imagination. The desired effect is to strike terror in the reader. The underlying ideas, however, are the sovereignty of God and of the Lamb, and God's desire to redirect sinful humankind. When people interpret various natural disasters as divine punishments and as signs of the impending end, how do you react? Is such thinking helpful or dangerous?

VII

Two Interludes and the Seventh Trumpet

Just as the series of seven seals was interrupted by two interludes (7:1-8, 9-17) between the sixth and seventh seals, so the series of seven trumpets is interrupted by two interludes (10:1-11; 11:1-14) between the sixth and seventh trumpets. The first interlude (10:1-11) is an encounter between the angel and the seer. The second interlude (11:1-14) concerns the "two witnesses." The seventh trumpet is described in 11:15-19.

The First Interlude: The Angel and the Prophet (10:1-11)

¹ Then I saw another mighty angel come down from heaven wrapped in a cloud, with a halo around his head; his face was like the sun and his feet were like pillars of fire. ² In his hand he held a small scroll that had been opened. He placed his right foot on the sea and his left foot on the land, ³ and then he cried out in a loud voice as a lion roars. When he cried out, the seven thunders raised their voices, too. ⁴ When the seven thunders had spoken, I was about to write it down; but I heard a voice from heaven say, "Seal up what the seven thunders have spoken, but do not write it down." ⁵ Then the angel I saw standing on the sea and on the land raised his right hand to heaven ⁶ and swore by the one who lives forever and ever, who created heaven and earth and sea and all

that is in them, "There shall be no more delay. [7] At the time when you hear the seventh angel blow his trumpet, the mysterious plan of God shall be fulfilled, as he promised to his servants the prophets."

[8] Then the voice that I heard from heaven spoke to me again and said, "Go, take the scroll that lies open in the hand of the angel who is standing on the sea and on the land." [9] So I went up to the angel and told him to give me the small scroll. He said to me, "Take and swallow it. It will turn your stomach sour, but in your mouth it will taste as sweet as honey." [10] I took the small scroll from the angel's hand and swallowed it. In my mouth it was like sweet honey, but when I had eaten it, my stomach turned sour. [11] Then someone said to me, "You must prophesy again about many peoples, nations, tongues, and kings."

The first interlude (10:1-11) assumes that the seer is on earth rather than in heaven (see 4:1). The scene is set in 10:1-4 with four figures or characters: the angel, the seven thunders, the voice, and the seer. Everything about the angel indicates dazzling brilliance: "wrapped in a cloud, with a halo around his head; his face was like the sun and his feet were like pillars of fire" (10:1). That one foot is on the sea and the other foot is on the land (10:2) indicates that the angel has significance for all the earth. The small scroll in his right hand (10:2) is the subject matter for the second part of the first interlude (10:8-11). The angel cries out "as a lion roars" (see Hos 11:10). The motif of the "seven thunders" is based on the seven references to the "voice of the LORD" in Psalm 29:3-9—an ancient description of God's power revealed in a thunderstorm. The seven thunders add noise to the glorious vision of the mighty angel. The "voice from heaven" (10:4; see also

10:8)—perhaps the voice of the risen Christ—tells John to seal up what the seven thunders said and not to write it down. What the seven thunders said, and why it should be sealed up and not written down, are not explained.

In 10:5-7 the gigantic and glorious angel becomes the focus of attention once more. He adopts the posture of one who takes a solemn oath ("raised his right hand to heaven") and swears by God the creator. Just as God created all things, so what follows will affect all creation. The angel's message is that "there shall be no more delay" (10:6). In other words, the fullness of God's kingdom and the series of events leading up to it will come soon—as soon as the sounding of the seventh trumpet (see 11:15-19). The "mysterious plan of God" (10:7) refers to God's ultimate purposes in guiding creation toward the fullness of God's reign (see 21:1-22:5). Whether the "prophets" refers to the biblical prophets (see especially Daniel 4, where "mystery" is a prominent expression for God's plan) or early Christian prophets, is not clear.

In 10:8-11 John is given the mission of a prophet. The scene evokes Ezekiel 3:1-4, where the prophet ("son of man") is told to eat the scroll that contains God's word before proclaiming it to the people. By ingesting the word, the prophet makes God's word his own and so is better able to proclaim it to Israel. Because the scroll contains God's word, it is "sweet as honey" in the prophet's mouth. As usual, the biblical model undergoes adaptation in the book of Revelation. First, the heavenly voice (10:8; see 10:4) instructs John to take the small scroll from the angel and to eat it. He then warns the seer that it will taste sour in his stomach (not found in Ezekiel 3:1-4) but sweet in his mouth (10:8-9). When John does as he is instructed

(10:10), he finds it to be exactly as the voice said it would be. The bitter-sweet combination probably refers to the contents of the scroll—a description of the future events that will entail much suffering (the "bitter"), and the promise of the vindication of the faithful witnesses and the divine judgment upon their wicked tormentors (the "sweet"). Having been commissioned as the biblical prophets were, John is told in 10:11 by "someone" to prophesy—to proclaim God's message to and for the peoples of the earth and their kings. His prophecy is not just for Israel. Rather, it pertains to all peoples of his world, including (and especially) the Romans and their emperor and the other rulers who did his bidding.

For Reflection: The two interludes and the description of the seventh trumpet are rich in biblical imagery that can occupy and stimulate the Christian imagination. Imagine yourself as John the seer now commissioned to be God's prophet and told to eat the little scroll. Taste how sweet it is in your mouth. Taste how bitter it is in your stomach. How do you understand the role of a prophet? Can you name some modern prophets? Was (or is) their role both sweet and bitter? Why?

The Two Witnesses (11:1-14)

[1] Then I was given a measuring rod like a staff and I was told, "Come and measure the temple of God and the altar, and count those who are worshiping in it. [2] But exclude the outer court of the temple; do not measure it, for it has been handed over to the Gentiles, who will trample the holy city for forty-two months. [3] I will commission my two witnesses to prophesy for those twelve

hundred and sixty days, wearing sackcloth." [4] These are the two olive trees and the two lampstands that stand before the Lord of the earth. [5] If anyone wants to harm them, fire comes out of their mouths and devours their enemies. In this way, anyone wanting to harm them is sure to be slain. [6] They have the power to close up the sky so that no rain can fall during the time of their prophesying. They also have power to turn water into blood and to afflict the earth with any plague as often as they wish.

[7] When they have finished their testimony, the beast that comes up from the abyss will wage war against them and conquer them and kill them. [8] Their corpses will lie in the main street of the great city, which has the symbolic names "Sodom" and "Egypt," where indeed their Lord was crucified. [9] Those from every people, tribe, tongue, and nation will gaze on their corpses for three and a half days, and they will not allow their corpses to be buried. [10] The inhabitants of the earth will gloat over them and be glad and exchange gifts because these two prophets tormented the inhabitants of the earth. [11] But after the three and a half days, a breath of life from God entered them. When they stood on their feet, great fear fell on those who saw them. [12] Then they heard a loud voice from heaven say to them, "Come up here." So they went up to heaven in a cloud as their enemies looked on. [13] At that moment there was a great earthquake, and a tenth of the city fell in ruins. Seven thousand people were killed during the earthquake; the rest were terrified and gave glory to the God of heaven.

[14] The second woe has passed, but the third is coming soon.

In the second interlude (11:1-13) John is told first to measure the inner court of the temple (11:1-2). Then he is told about the two witnesses (11:3-6), the fate that will befall them (11:7-10), and their resurrection and vindication (11:11-13). This is identified in 11:14 as the "second woe" (see 9:12). The passage is full of allusions to the Old Testament but (as always in Revelation) there are many adaptations and developments to fit the situation of the Christian communities in the late first century.

Like the prophets Ezekiel (see Ez 40:3–42:20; 47:1-12) and Zechariah (see Zec 2:5-6), John in 11:1-2 is given a measuring rod and told to "measure the temple of God." But here the temple of God is not the Jerusalem temple. Rather, it seems to be the Christian community, the people of God ("those who are worshiping"). The measuring serves to protect them against the destructive forces that threaten them with harm. Those forces have possession of the outer court—the equivalent to the Court of the Gentiles in the Jerusalem temple. Those forces will control the world and "trample the holy city" (11:2) for forty-two months or three and a half years—just as the Seleucid King Antiochus IV Epiphanes had control over Jerusalem and its temple between 167 and 164 B.C. (see Dn 7:25; 12:7). The idea is that the great persecution will be limited in time and God will protect the faithful people of God and finally vindicate them.

During the 1,260 days of persecution (see Dn 12:7) God will raise up "two witnesses" (11:3) whose task ("to prophesy") and life-style ("wearing sackcloth") place them in line with the biblical prophets. Are these two witnesses historical figures of the recent past (such as the martyrs Peter and Paul) or future figures? Whatever their precise identity may be, they are presented in terms of biblical models. First, in 11:4 they are described as "two olive trees" (anointed ones) and as "the two lampstands," thus evoking the biblical descriptions of the post-exilic high priest Joshua and the Jewish governor Zerubbabel (see Zec 4:3, 11, 14). Then in 11:5-6 they are portrayed in terms of Elijah and Moses. Elijah called down fire from heaven (see 2 Kgs 1:10) and closed up the heavens so that it would not rain (see 1 Kgs 17:1). So the two witnesses, according to 11:5-6a, send forth fire from their mouths and close up the sky. Moses turned water into blood (see Ex 7:17-20) and brought all kinds of plagues against the enemies of God's people. So the two witnesses will protect God's people for a time against the attacks of their enemies (11:6b).

The two witnesses, according to 11:7-10, suffer martyrdom under "the beast that comes up from the abyss" (11:7). When this "beast" is identified as the emperor Nero (as seems likely), there is further support for identifying the two witnesses as Peter and Paul, who suffered martyrdom during Nero's persecution of Christians in the sixties of the first century. Their death occurs in "the great city" (11:8). In various texts in Revelation (see 14:8; 16:19; 17:18; 18:2, 10, 21) that expression is used for Babylon, the city whose armies destroyed Jerusalem in the sixth century B.C. and forced its leaders into exile. In Revelation, however, and elsewhere (see 1 Pt 5:13), it is undoubtedly a code-word for Rome. The wickedness of the great city is further emphasized by the symbolic names "Sodom" (see Gn 18:16–19:29) and "Egypt" (the place of ancient Israel's captivity according to Exodus 1–15). And even though Jesus was crucified in Jerusalem, the ultimate legal responsibility lay with the Roman prefect Pontius Pilate. And so it can be said that Jesus too was put to death in "Rome." According to 11:9-10, the inhabitants of the Roman empire will gloat over the deaths of the two witnesses and imagine them to have been defeated definitively. That their corpses are left unburied for three and half days (see 11:9, 11) adds to the insults already visited upon the two witnesses.

The vindication of the two witnesses (11:11-14) takes the form of their resuscitation/resurrection and exaltation to God's heavenly court. The language describing their resuscitation/resurrection evokes the creation story of Genesis (see Gn 2:7; 6:17; 7:15, 22) and the prophet Ezekiel's vision of national resurrection in the valley of the "dry bones" (see Ez 37:1-14). Just as the prophet Elijah (see 2 Kgs 2:11) and Moses (see Dt 34:6), as well as Enoch (see Gn 5:24), were taken up into heaven, so the two witnesses are taken up into the divine court. The glee of their enemies turns to terror not only at the spectacle of the vindication of the two witnesses but also at the great earthquake that follows (11:13; see also Ezekiel 38:19-20, where a great earthquake follows the prophet's vision of national "resurrection"). The seven thousand persons killed in the earthquake are representative figures (seven times a thousand). As in 9:20-21, the purpose of the cosmic catastrophes is to lead people to repent. The event is identified as the "second woe" (see 9:2), with still one more to come (see 11:15-19).

For Reflection: Imagine yourself as part of God's people—measured and protected against the hostility of your persecutors. How might you feel? Imagine yourself as a witness to the career of the two witnesses—to their witness on behalf of God's people, their tragic deaths, and their vindication by God. What might you see and hear? How might you feel?

The Seventh Trumpet (11:15-19)

15 Then the seventh angel blew his trumpet. There were loud voices in heaven, saying, "The kingdom of the world now belongs to our Lord and to his Anointed, and he will reign forever and ever." 16 The twenty-four elders who sat on their thrones before God prostrated themselves and worshiped God 17 and said:

"We give thanks to you, Lord God almighty,
who are and who were.
For you have assumed your great power
and have established your reign.
18 The nations raged,
but your wrath has come,
and the time for the dead to be judged,
and to recompense your servants, the prophets,
and the holy ones and those who fear your name,
the small and the great alike,
and to destroy those who destroy the earth."

19 Then God's temple in heaven was opened, and the ark of his covenant could be seen in the temple. There were flashes of lightning, rumblings, and peals of thunder, an earthquake, and violent hailstorm.

The sounding of the seventh trumpet signals the end of the present evil age and the coming of the fullness of God's kingdom (see 10:6, "There shall be no more delay"). Whereas the seventh seal was accompanied by "silence in heaven for about half an hour" (8:1), the seventh trumpet is accompanied by loud voices (11:15), the chorus of the twenty-four elders (11:16-18), and a "sound and light" show in heaven (11:19).

The scene is set in heaven. The "loud voices" in 11:15 proclaim that with the seventh trumpet the fullness of God's kingdom will come. That kingdom belongs "to our

Lord and to his Anointed" (see Ps 2:2). Once more God and Jesus the Lamb are placed on the same level, and both are probably included as the subject of "he will reign forever and ever."

The twenty-four elders show proper reverence to God (11:16), proclaim God's reign (11:17), and outline some of the events associated with the coming of that reign in its fullness (11:18). They first thank the "Lord God almighty," for the Eternal One ("who are and who were") will have established his kingdom in its fullness. This will be the answer to Jesus' own prayer: "Thy kingdom come" (Mt 6:10; Lk 11:2). Then in 11:18 they focus on some events related to the kingdom's coming: the rebelliousness of the nations, the coming of God's wrath, and the last judgment. This sequence corresponds not only to what is described in the second half of Revelation but also to what appears in the Synoptic "little apocalypse" (Mk 13; Mt 24–25; Lk 21). The result of God's final judgment will be vindication for the righteous faithful and destruction for the human and superhuman enemies of God's people ("those who destroy the earth").

In 11:19a the fullness of God's kingdom is celebrated by the opening of God's temple in heaven and the manifestation of the ark of the covenant. Both the Jerusalem temple and the ark were signs of God's presence in Israel. But the ark was lost in the destruction of the First Temple, and the Second Temple was destroyed by the Romans in A.D. 70. These earthly entities, however, were at best signs of the heavenly realities to be revealed when God's kingdom comes. (Note that in the new Jerusalem, according to 21:22, there is no temple.)

The "sound and light" show (11:19b) is reminiscent of the cosmic events accompanying the giving of the Law on Mount Sinai (see Ex 19:16). It is the language of theophany—the manifestation of God's presence that produces awe and fear among those who are anywhere near it. The display is linked to the elders' celebration of the establishment of God's reign (see 11:17). When the seventh trumpet has been sounded, the second sequence of end-time events is complete. The second series is probably best viewed as parallel, rather than subsequent, to the first series of seven seals. In other words, both sequences describe the events leading up to the full coming of God's kingdom and the vindication of the righteous faithful.

For Reflection: Imagine yourself hearing the sounding of the seventh trumpet, as well as the songs proclaiming the kingdom of God and celebrating the triumph of the Lamb. Imagine yourself seeing and hearing the heavenly "sound and light" show. What might you hear and see? What overall emotional and intellectual impact does the whole sequence of the seven trumpets have on you?

VIII

The Woman and the Dragon

The beginning of the central section in the book of Revelation (chaps. 12–14) features two descriptions of the conflict between the woman and the dragon (12:1-6, 13-18), placed around the account of the archangel Michael's victory over the dragon (12:7-12). The woman personifies the people of God, and her child is the Messiah. The dragon is Satan, the serpent of Genesis 3 (see 12:9).

The Two Signs (12:1-6)

¹ A great sign appeared in the sky, a woman clothed with the sun, with the moon under her feet, and on her head a crown of twelve stars. ² She was with child and wailed aloud in pain as she labored to give birth. ³ Then another sign appeared in the sky; it was a huge red dragon, with seven heads and ten horns, and on its heads were seven diadems. ⁴ Its tail swept away a third of the stars in the sky and hurled them down to the earth. Then the dragon stood before the woman about to give birth, to devour her child when she gave birth. ⁵ She gave birth to a son, a male child, destined to rule all the nations with an iron rod. Her child was caught up to God and his throne. ⁶ The woman herself fled into the desert where she had a place prepared by God, that there she

might be taken care of for twelve hundred and sixty days.

The "great sign" (12:1-2) is the woman who is about to give birth. Though various elements in her description can be traced to Greek and other mythology (see also Gn 37:9), in this context the figure represents (the new) Israel as the people of God. The identification of her as Mary the Mother of Jesus is a secondary development, though not an inappropriate one, since Mary is the mother of the Messiah and personifies the people of God. In giving birth to the Messiah the pregnant woman (see Is 7:14) endures the birth-pangs associated with child-bearing since Genesis 3:16.

The "other sign" (12:3-4a) features the dragon—the mythical monster identified elsewhere as Rahab (see Ps 89:11; Jb 26:12-13) and Leviathan (see Ps 74:13-14). In 12:9 (see also 20:2) the dragon is further identified as the Devil and Satan as well as the Serpent of Genesis 3. The dragon is the great personification of evil, the one who stands behind the evils that happen on earth and are now afflicting the churches of western Asia Minor addressed in Revelation. The seven heads and the ten horns (see Dn 7:8, 24) and ten crowns signify how powerful a force and how wide a rule the dragon has. So powerful is the dragon that its tail sweeps a third of the stars down to earth (see Dn 8:10, 12).

The two signs come together in 12:4b-6 as the woman gives birth to the child and the dragon tries to destroy the child. From the Christian perspective, the child is the Messiah Jesus who is born from Israel/the people of God/Mary. The child is described in terms of the messianic figure in Psalm 2: "destined to rule all the nations with an iron rod" (see 2:27; 19:15). The dragon, however, is foiled when the child is brought up to God and his throne—a description of the exaltation or ascension of Jesus. Note that in this scene there is reference only to the Messiah's birth and exaltation. The woman, who is now clearly the church (in which the identity of God's people continues), finds safety in the desert place prepared by God (divine protection) for 1,260 days (a fairly short time; see Dn 7:25; 12:7; Rv 11:3).

For Reflection: This scene enables the readers to locate themselves in God's plan. Jesus the risen and exalted Messiah has escaped the dragon's power. The church on earth now enjoys at least a temporary protection as it awaits the full manifestation of God's kingdom. What understanding of Jesus does this text present? How might it help Christians in facing persecution?

The Cosmic Battle (12:7-12)

⁷ Then the war broke out in heaven; Michael and his angels battled against the dragon. The dragon and its angels fought back, ⁸ but they did not prevail and there was no longer any place for them in heaven. ⁹ The huge dragon, the ancient serpent, who is called the Devil and Satan, who deceived the whole world, was thrown down to earth, and its angels were thrown down with it.
¹⁰ Then I heard a loud voice in heaven say:
"Now have salvation and power come,
 and the kingdom of our God
 and the authority of his Anointed.
For the accuser of our brothers is cast out,
 who accuses them before our God day and night.

¹¹ They conquered him by the blood of the Lamb
and by the word of their testimony;
love for life did not deter them from death.
¹² Therefore, rejoice, you heavens,
and you who dwell in them.
But woe to you, earth and sea,
for the Devil has come down to you in great fury,
for he knows he has but a short time."

The narrative of the woman and the dragon is interrupted in 12:7-12 by the report of a cosmic battle (12:7-9)
and a song of celebration (12:10-12). The battle takes
place in heaven between Michael and the dragon. Michael
the archangel is the traditional guardian of God's people
(see Dn 10:13, 21; 12:1). The dragon in 12:9 is identified
and connected with the ancient serpent of Genesis 3, as
well as the Devil and Satan (see Job 1; but Satan here is a
much more negative figure). (The battle between Michael
and Satan is also described in the *War Scroll* among the
Dead Sea scrolls.) Michael and his forces prevail over the
dragon and its forces (12:8). The result is that the dragon
and its forces are thrown out of heaven. But since they are
thrown down to earth, this means that the faithful on
earth are now vulnerable to their attacks (12:9).

The song of celebration in 12:10-12 takes place in
heaven but probably comes not from angels but rather
from the martyrs who have already been glorified (see
6:11) as "the accuser of our brothers" suggests. The sing-
ers attribute the victory to God and his Messiah, again
placing the two figures on the same level. The description
of Satan as the "accuser of our brothers" is based ultimately on the figure who in Job 1 serves as a kind of prose-
cuting attorney in the heavenly court. The middle verse

101

(12:11) focuses more on the martyrs' victory than on Michael's victory. That victory is attributed to the "blood of the Lamb"—Jesus' death—and to the witness of the martyrs who remain faithful. The hymn ends in 12:12 with a call for all creation to join in the celebration ("rejoice, you heavens and you who dwell in them") as well as with a caution to the earth and sea because now the devil/dragon still has the power to inflict evil there for at least a short time.

For Reflection: Again this text can help the readers to understand their situation. The ultimate victory over evil and Satan has been won by God, the Lamb, and Michael and his angels. Satan, however, still has some limited power to harm God's people on earth. But that is only for a short time, and therefore the proper response on the part of God's people is faithful witness. How might this vision encourage God's people today?

The Battle on Earth (12:13-18)

13 When the dragon saw that it had been thrown down to the earth, it pursued the woman who had given birth to the male child. 14 But the woman was given the two wings of the great eagle, so that she could fly to her place in the desert, where, far from the serpent, she was taken care of for a year, two years, and a half-year. 15 The serpent, however, spewed a torrent of water out of his mouth after the woman to sweep her away with the current. 16 But the earth helped the woman and opened its mouth and swallowed the flood that the dragon spewed out of its mouth. 17 Then the dragon became angry with the woman and went off to wage war against the rest of her offspring, those who keep God's commandments

and bear witness to Jesus. [18] It took its position on the sand of the sea.

The narrative of the woman and the dragon is resumed in 12:13-18. Since the dragon had been defeated in heaven and cast down to earth, it pursues the mother of the Messiah (the people of God, understood now as the Church). But according to 12:14, God grants to the Church the means of escape ("the two wings of the great eagle," see Ex 19:4; Dt 32:11; Is 40:3) at least for the limited duration of the struggle ("for a year, two years, and a half-year," see Dn 7:25; 12:7). When the serpent/dragon continues to pursue the woman/Church in 12:15-16, the earth itself takes the woman's side and swallows up the torrent of water sent forth by the dragon. Frustrated by his failure to destroy the child/Messiah and the woman/Church, the dragon in 12:17 turns to the Christians on earth—those who are addressed by the book of Revelation as a whole. These are defined as "those who keep God's commandments and bear witness to Jesus"—the Christian ideal according to Revelation.

The description of the dragon (reading "it" rather than "I") as taking its position on the sand of the sea in 12:18 serves as the setting for introducing the other two members of the "unholy trinity": the beast from the sea (13:1) and the other beast from the earth (13:11). These three figures represent the enemies of God's people in the present.

For Reflection: Revelation 12 is bursting with marvelous images. At each verse one can stop and reflect on what is seen and heard: the woman about to give birth, the dragon who tries to kill her newborn son, the battle in the heavens

103

between Michael and the dragon, the song of victory, the dragon's pursuit of the woman, and his attempt to destroy God's people on earth. At the same time, one must not neglect the theological claims of the passage: God's ultimate victory over evil has been won through the "blood of the Lamb"; the Messiah has escaped the dragon's attack and is enthroned with God in heaven; and the persecution of those who keep God's commandments and bear witness to Jesus is limited in time and will issue in their final vindication. Does this text help you to locate yourself and the people of God today in the history of salvation? Why, or why not?

IX
The Two Beasts

The descriptions of the two beasts in 13:1-10 and
13:11-18 clarify greatly the situation that the book of
Revelation originally addressed. The beast from the sea
represents the Roman emperor, and the beast from the
land represents the local official in Asia Minor, who was
promoting worship of the emperor and thus causing the
crisis of conscience faced by the Christians addressed in
Revelation.

The Beast from the Sea (13:1-10)

[1] Then I saw a beast come out of the sea with ten
horns and seven heads; on its horns were ten diadems,
and on its heads blasphemous name[s]. [2] The beast I saw
was like a leopard, but it had feet like a bear's, and its
mouth was like the mouth of a lion. To it the dragon
gave its own power and throne, along with great authority. [3] I saw that one of its heads seemed to have been
mortally wounded, but this mortal wound was healed.
Fascinated, the whole world followed after the beast.
[4] They worshiped the dragon because it gave its authority to the beast; they also worshiped the beast and said,
"Who can compare with the beast or who can fight
against it?"
[5] The beast was given a mouth uttering proud boasts
and blasphemies, and it was given authority to act for

forty-two months. ⁶ It opened its mouth to utter blasphemies against God, blaspheming his name and his dwelling and those who dwell in heaven. ⁷ It was also allowed to wage war against the holy ones and conquer them, and it was granted authority over every tribe, people, tongue, and nation. ⁸ All the inhabitants of the earth will worship it, all whose names were not written from the foundation of the world in the book of life, which belongs to the Lamb who was slain.

⁹ Whoever has ears ought to hear these words.

¹⁰ Anyone destined for captivity goes into captivity.

Anyone destined to be slain by the sword shall be slain by the sword.

Such is the faithful endurance of the holy ones.

The beast from the sea (13:1-2) is described in terms taken from Daniel 7: The beast comes from the sea (Dn 7:2-3), has ten horns (Dn 7:8, 24), and has the features of a leopard, a bear, and a lion (Dn 7:4-6). Originally used in connection with the Seleucid King Antiochus IV Epiphanes—the great enemy of Israel in the second century B.C., these features are here attributed to a Roman emperor in the late first century A.D. The most likely candidate is the emperor Domitian (who reigned from A.D. 81 to 96), though there are features of Nero (who reigned from A.D. 54 to 68). This transfer reflects a shift in interpreting the fourth of the four empires in Daniel 2 from Greece to Rome. The ten horns and ten diadems may refer to the series of Roman emperors (see 17:10, 12-14). The "blasphemous names" allude to the divine titles attributed to and/or demanded by Roman emperors—titles such as lord, god, august one, divine, and so forth. The source of the beast's power is the dragon (13:2b), and so the beast from the sea (across the Mediterranean Sea from

Asia Minor) is the second member of the "unholy trinity" empowered by Satan.

The head that was "mortally wounded" (13:3) was most likely the emperor Nero, since there were rumors that he had not actually died but had been restored to life. John interprets the fascination aroused by such rumors as the cause of recent interest in worshiping the emperor as divine. The emperor who seemed to have been mortally wounded but restored to life is the antithesis of the "Lamb that seemed to have been slain" (see 5:6) and truly had been restored to life. According to 13:4, worship of the dragon (Satan) and worship of the beast (the Roman emperor) are linked. Those who worship the beast imagine that he is incomparable and invincible. They say: "Who can compare with the beast or who can fight against it?" John's response is, "The Lamb that seemed to have been slain."

The activities of the beast from the sea (13:5-8) are also described in terms of Daniel 7: The beast utters "proud boasts and blasphemies" (Dn 7:8, 11); his authority lasts only for the limited period of "forty-two months" (Dn 7:25); he utters "blasphemies against God" (Dn 7:25) and against the heavenly court; and he is allowed to wage "war against the holy ones" (Dn 7:21). The result is persecution against God's people (Rv 13:7). All the world (the Roman empire) participates in the worship of the Roman emperor—all except those who remain the faithful witnesses to the Lamb, the very ones whom John is trying to affirm and encourage to remain faithful. The "book of life" (a common motif in Jewish apocalyptic writings) is here said to belong to the Lamb (Jesus) who was slain, and not to the emperor (Nero) who "seemed to have been mortally wounded" (13:3).

How is the Christian community to respond to the persecution from the beast? It is to do so with faithful endurance (see 13:10b) rather than with violent resistance. After the call to hear (13:9), familiar from the letters to the seven churches (2:7, 11, 17, 29; 3:6, 13, 22), there is a plea for patient acceptance of captivity and even death (see Jer 15:2; 43:11).

For Reflection: This patient acceptance is based on the theological conviction that the ultimate victory has been won already by the slain Lamb, that the dragon and his beasts have only limited and temporary power, and that soon the faithful witnesses will be vindicated and become part of the heavenly court. These theological convictions made possible the loyal endurance of the "holy ones" in the persecution. Are you convinced that you belong to Jesus the slain Lamb so much that you would endure captivity or even death for the sake of the gospel?

The Beast from the Land (13:11-18)

> [11] Then I saw another beast come up out of the earth; it had two horns like a lamb's but spoke like a dragon. [12] It wielded all the authority of the first beast in its sight and made the earth and its inhabitants worship the first beast, whose mortal wound had been healed. [13] It performed great signs, even making fire come down from heaven to earth in the sight of everyone. [14] It deceived the inhabitants of the earth with the signs it was allowed to perform in the sight of the first beast, telling them to make an image for the beast who had been wounded by the sword and revived. [15] It was then per-

mitted to breathe life into the beast's image, so that the beast's image could speak and [could] have anyone who did not worship it put to death. [16] It forced all the people, small and great, rich and poor, free and slave, to be given a stamped image on their right hands or their foreheads, [17] so that no one could buy or sell except one who had the stamped image of the beast's name or the number that stood for its name.

[18] Wisdom is needed here; one who understands can calculate the number of the beast, for it is a number that stands for a person. His number is six hundred and sixty-six.

The second beast (13:11-12) comes up "out of the earth" (13:11), indicating that this is a local figure from the area addressed in the letters to the seven churches in western Asia Minor, as opposed to the first beast (the Roman emperor) who comes from "the sea." The second beast is most likely a local official—a governor or perhaps a powerful pagan priest—who was eagerly promoting worship of the emperor and of the goddess Roma (the personification of Rome). Elsewhere he is called the "false prophet" (see Rv 16:13; 19:20; 20:10). Though in appearance he may look like a lamb (see Matthew 7:15, and compare the portrayal of Jesus as the slain Lamb in Revelation), the second beast is a creature of the dragon (Satan) and does the dragon's bidding (13:11). He also does the bidding of the first beast (the Roman emperor), and so tries to promote the cult of the emperor by making "the earth and its inhabitants worship the first beast" (13:12). The description of the emperor as one "whose mortal wound had been healed" once more seems to evoke the rumor that Nero had been restored to life (see 13:3).

The description of the emperor cult in 13:13-15 gives precious insight into the particular situation addressed in the book as a whole. The "great signs" (see Mk 13:22; 2 Thes 2:9) included making fire come down (13:13) and making statues speak by ventriloquism (13:15), both gimmicks designed to startle and impress a gullible audience. That the worship focuses on the emperor is indicated by 13:14, where the first beast is again described in terms of Nero restored to life: "the beast who had been wounded by the sword and revived." The penalty for failure to participate in emperor worship was apparently death: Anyone who did not worship it was to be "put to death" (13:15).

Those who worship the beast belong to the beast (13:16-18). All of them bear his "stamped image" on their right hands and foreheads (13:16). In this way they show that they are the emperor's property and that they regard him as their lord. But the central claim of Revelation is that God (and the slain Lamb), not the emperor, is Lord. The reference to bearing the stamped image may allude to the Jewish practice of wearing phylacteries on the right arm and on the head to indicate belonging to God. It surely alludes, from the reader's perspective, to the sealing of the 144,000 faithful witnesses (see 7:1-8). Moreover, the devotees of the emperor use the emperor's coinage to buy and sell (see Mk 12:13-17).

The stamp consists of the name of the beast and his number—which in this case are the same. The number according to 13:18 is 666. Each unit in the number falls below the "perfect" number seven that is so prominent throughout Revelation, and thus reinforces the idea of the beast's imperfection. The number 666 refers most directly to the emperor Nero. The number is the result of adding the letters in Nero's name and title. When Nero's Greek name is transliterated into Hebrew characters as NRWN QSR ("Nero Caesar") and those Hebrew letters are given their numerical values (N = 50, R = 200, W = 6, N = 50, Q = 100, S = 60, R = 200), the total is 666.

For Reflection: The descriptions of the two beasts call for "wisdom" (see 13:18) on the modern reader's part. There are many exotic images and obscure statements. And yet the situation—the persecution of Christians for their efforts at remaining faithful to the worship of God and of the Lamb—is something that Christians have faced in every generation somewhere and still do today. Read again through the descriptions of the two beasts and the events associated with them, and imagine yourself faced with the choice whether to go along with most other people or to resist. Do you ever pray for those who now suffer persecution for their faith? Do you ever take steps to get such persons freed or at least to alleviate their sufferings?

X
A Preview of the End

The preview of the end presented in 14:1-20 rounds off the central section (chaps. 12–14) of the book. Whereas chapters 12 and 13 portray the threat posed by the "unholy trinity" of the dragon and the two beasts to the people of God on earth, chapter 14 anticipates how the evil forces will be judged and the faithful witnesses vindicated. It first presents a vision of the Lamb's companions and gives an interpretation (14:1-5). Then three angels proclaim judgment against the enemies of God's people (14:6-13), and the end is described in terms of the biblical images of the harvest and the winepress (14:14-20).

The Lamb and His Companions (14:1-5)

¹ Then I looked and there was the Lamb standing on Mount Zion, and with him a hundred and forty-four thousand who had his name and his Father's name written on their foreheads. ² I heard a sound from heaven like the sound of rushing water or a loud peal of thunder. The sound I heard was like that of harpists playing their harps. ³ They were singing [what seemed to be] a new hymn before the throne, before the four living creatures and the elders. No one could learn this hymn except the hundred and forty-four thousand who had been ransomed from the earth. ⁴ These are they who were not defiled with women; they are virgins and these

are the ones who follow the Lamb wherever he goes. They have been ransomed as the first-fruits of the human race for God and the Lamb. ⁵On their lips no deceit has been found; they are unblemished.

The Lamb standing on Mount Zion (14:1) functions as the antithesis of the beast from the sea (13:1). According to Joel 3:5, Mount Zion is the place of divine deliverance. His 144,000 companions (see 7:1-17) bear the names of the Lamb and the Father on their foreheads, and so they are the antithesis of those who bear the image and name of the beast (see 13:16-18). The sound that John hears (14:2-3) comes from heaven. It is compared in turn to rushing water, a peal of thunder, and harp music. It is a "new hymn" because it celebrates the new act of God about to take place in the final judgment. Only those who show that they belong to God and the Lamb by their faithful witness—the 144,000 "ransomed from the earth"—can learn the heavenly hymn.

The identity of the 144,000 is clarified in 14:4-5. It is very likely that the sexual imagery here ("not defiled with women . . . virgins") refers metaphorically to the refusal of the 144,000 to participate in the worship of the emperor and the goddess Roma. The imagery presupposes the common biblical motif of idolatry as adultery or fornication. By their faithful witness the 144,000 martyrs have followed the Lamb as far as death. Thus they represent the "first-fruits" and the "unblemished" sacrifice to God. Just as the Lamb's death was a sacrifice, so is their death. Their refusal to deny their faith and to participate in emperor worship is an indication of their total integrity: "On their lips no deceit has been found."

For Reflection: The faithful witnesses are models of integrity. They refuse to compromise their beliefs, even if it costs them their lives. Can you think of examples of such integrity in recent history or in your own experience? How do you define integrity?

The Three Angels' Proclamation (14:6-13)

⁶ Then I saw another angel flying overhead, with everlasting good news to announce to those who dwell on earth, to every nation, tribe, tongue, and people. ⁷ He said in a loud voice, "Fear God and give him glory, for his time has come to sit in judgment. Worship him who made heaven and earth and sea and springs of water."
⁸ A second angel followed, saying:
"Fallen, fallen is Babylon the great,
   that made all the nations drink
   the wine of her licentious passion."
⁹ A third angel followed them and said in a loud voice, "Anyone who worships the beast or its image, or accepts its mark on forehead or hand, ¹⁰ will also drink the wine of God's fury, poured full strength into the cup of his wrath, and will be tormented in burning sulfur before the holy angels and before the Lamb. ¹¹ The smoke of the fire that torments them will rise forever and ever, and there will be no relief day or night for those who worship the beast or its image or accept the mark of its name." ¹² Here is what sustains the holy ones who keep God's commandments and their faith in Jesus.
¹³ I heard a voice from heaven say, "Write this: Blessed are the dead who die in the Lord from now on." "Yes," said the Spirit, "let them find rest from their labors, for their works accompany them."

The three angels in 14:6-13 proclaim judgment against the enemies of God's people. The first angel (14:6-7) announces the coming judgment as "everlasting good news" (for the faithful witnesses). The audience for his message is all the inhabitants of the earth. The content of the message is that "his time has come to sit in judgment" and that the appropriate responses are to "fear God and give him glory," and to worship him as creator and lord of the universe.

The second angel (14:8) proclaims the fall of Babylon (see Is 21:9; Jer 51:8; here the code name for Rome). The "wine of her licentious passion" describes Rome's seductive power (see also 17:2; 18:3) over all the peoples of the empire.

The third angel (14:9-11) proclaims eternal punishment upon those who worship the beast/emperor. Those who participate in emperor worship and accept the emperor as lord (14:9b) will drink the "wine of God's fury" (14:10a)—a variation on the biblical motif of the cup of suffering or of God's wrath (see Is 51:17; Jer 25:15-16; 49:12; etc.). In antiquity wine was generally mixed with water before it was drunk. But the wine of God's fury will be poured "full strength." Another motif to express the punishment of the emperor's followers is "burning sulfur," which is literally "fire and brimstone" (see Is 39:8-10; Gn 19:24). What is described is the state of the condemned at the last judgment. Their punishment takes place in the sight of the angels and the Lamb, and apparently goes on without end (14:11).

The punishment of the wicked is conversely the vindication of the righteous and the proof of God's justice. The law of retribution states that the righteous are rewarded and the wicked are punished according to their deeds. The apocalyptic perspective holds that, despite appearances in the present, this law is still in force and is upheld at the last judgment (see also the book of Daniel). Belief in God's justice is what sustains "the holy ones who keep God's commandments and their faith in Jesus" (14:12). The beatitude issued by the heavenly voice in 14:13a declares happy or blessed those "who die in the Lord"—the faithful witnesses to the Lamb. The response from the Spirit in 14:13b interprets the martyrs' death as "rest from their labors." Since "their works accompany them," they have nothing to fear in the last judgment—which in fact will represent their complete vindication.

For Reflection: The preview of the end in chapter 14 is intended to instill hope among God's faithful people. The slain Lamb, not the emperor, is the lord. Those who share his sacrificial death will share his eternal life. The divine judgment upon Rome and the followers of the beast will be the definitive manifestation of God's justice. The wicked will receive the punishments that they deserve, and the righteous will be vindicated and rewarded as their faithful witness deserves. Do you find a tension between the justice of God and the mercy of God?

The Harvest (14:14-20)

14 Then I looked and there was a white cloud, and sitting on the cloud one who looked like a son of man, with a gold crown on his head and a sharp sickle in his hand. 15 Another angel came out of the temple, crying out in a loud voice to the one sitting on the cloud, "Use your sickle and reap the harvest, for the time to reap has come, because the earth's harvest is fully ripe." 16 So the one who was sitting on the cloud swung his sickle over the earth, and the earth was harvested.

[17] Then another angel came out of the temple in heaven who also had a sharp sickle. [18] Then another angel [came] from the altar, [who] was in charge of the fire, and cried out in a loud voice to the one who had the sharp sickle, "Use your sharp sickle and cut the clusters from the earth's vines, for its grapes are ripe." [19] So the angel swung his sickle over the earth and cut the earth's vintage. He threw it into the great wine press of God's fury. [20] The wine press was trodden outside the city and blood poured out of the wine press to the height of a horse's bridle for two hundred miles.

The central section (chaps. 12–14) closes with two scenes of the last judgment under the image of a harvest (14:14-16, 17-20). In the first scene one "like a son of man" (see Dn 7:13) is told by an angel coming from the heavenly temple to use his sickle and reap the harvest. The angel uses the language of Joel 4:13, and the one "like a son of man" (the risen Jesus?) swings his sickle and brings in the harvest. For the last judgment as a harvest see the parable of the wheat and the weeds in Matthew 13:24-30, 36-43 (see also Jl 3:13; Hos 6:11; Jer 51:33; etc.).

The second judgment scene (14:17-20) features an angel in place of the one "like a son of man." He too wields a sharp sickle as in Joel 4:13. But here the imagery of the winepress and the blood (like the grape-juice) is taken from Isaiah 63:1-6. The vineyard is harvested (see the parable of the vineyard in Matthew 21:33-46), and the grapes are thrown "into the great wine press of God's fury" (14:19). The result is much blood everywhere ("to the height of a horse's bridle for two hundred miles")—an indication of how many wicked persons populate the earth. The carnage, however, takes place "outside the city," which is most likely the new Jerusalem inhabited by God, the Lamb, the angels, and the holy ones who have remained faithful.

For Reflection: The final judgment (the "harvest") will involve the definitive separation between the righteous and the wicked. How would this idea have encouraged "the holy ones?" Does it encourage you? Or does it discourage you?

XI
The Seven Bowls

As with the seven seals (6:1–8:1) and the seven trumpets (8:2–11:19), the seven bowls (16:1-21) bring punishment upon those who worship the beast and blaspheme against God. Chapter 15 introduces the seven angels who will pour out the seven bowls of God's wrath.

The Angels (15:1-8)

[1] Then I saw in heaven another sign, great and awe-inspiring: seven angels with the seven last plagues, for through them God's fury is accomplished.

[2] Then I saw something like a sea of glass mingled with fire. On the sea of glass were standing those who had won the victory over the beast and its image and the number that signified its name. They were holding God's harps, [3] and they sang the song of Moses, the servant of God, and the song of the Lamb:
"Great and wonderful are your works,
   Lord God almighty.
Just and true are your ways,
   O king of the nations.
[4] Who will not fear you, Lord,
   or glorify your name?
For you alone are holy.
All the nations will come
   and worship before you,
for your righteous acts have been revealed."

⁵ After this I had another vision. The temple that is the heavenly tent of testimony opened, ⁶ and the seven angels with the seven plagues came out of the temple. They were dressed in clean white linen, with a gold sash around their chests. ⁷ One of the four living creatures gave the seven angels seven gold bowls filled with the fury of God, who lives forever and ever. ⁸ Then the temple became so filled with the smoke from God's glory and might that no one could enter it until the seven plagues of the seven angels had been accomplished.

Chapter 15 consists of three visions, each one introduced by "And I saw" (15:1, 2, 5). The first vision (15:1) concerns the "seven angels with the seven last plagues." The term "plague" here refers not to infectious diseases but rather to the "blows" or disasters visited upon the wicked. These plagues will bring to full measure the wrath of God (though the book moves on into chapter 17 after the seven bowls of wrath have been poured out). The seven angels are also the subject of the third vision in the series (15:5-8).

The second vision (15:2-4) features "a sea of glass" (a symbol of peace and tranquility in 4:6) "mingled with fire" (a symbol of the struggles and trials that the martyrs have endured). What is on the sea of glass— those who conquered the beast (the Roman emperor), its image (a statue of him), and the number signifying his name (666 = NRWN QSR = Nero Caesar, see 13:18)—represents the victory of those who have remained faithful witnesses. The conquerors play God's harps and sing a song of victory. The "song of Moses" (see Ex 15:1-18) and the "song of the Lamb" celebrate the triumphs of God first in the exodus from Egypt, then in Jesus' death and resurrection, and finally in the full manifestation of God's kingdom.

The reference to the song of Moses prepares also for the seven plagues in chapter 16, which are strongly influenced by events associated with the exodus from Egypt.

The individual phrases in the song (15:3b-4) come from various parts of the Old Testament: "Great and wonderful are your works" (Ps 111:2; 139:4); "just and true are your ways" (Ps 145:17; Dt 32:4); and so forth. The song praises the works and words of God (15:3b), asks how anyone could fail to fear or glorify God (15:4a), and looks to all the nations to acknowledge God as the holy one (15:4b). What is celebrated is that God's "righteous acts" or "just judgments" have been (or will soon be) revealed. These just judgments refer to the events leading up to the last judgment and to the last judgment itself.

The third vision (15:5-8) again features the seven angels (see 15:1). It takes place in the heavenly temple. The overloaded expression "the temple that is the heavenly tent of testimony" (15:5) evokes various images that point to the special place of God's presence. Of course, God is even more powerfully present in the heavenly court than anywhere on earth. The seven angels with the seven plagues (15:6) come forth from the heavenly temple, dressed much as the risen Christ was described in 1:13. Their white linen garments and gold sashes indicate that they share the victory of the Lamb.

The seven angels receive the seven gold bowls (15:7) from one of the "four living creatures" inhabiting the heavenly court (see 4:6-8). These bowls are meant to be instruments of God's wrath and will carry out God's just judgments against the wicked. For the temple filled with the smoke (or cloud) of God's glory in 15:8, see Ezekiel 10:4 and Exodus 40:35. No one could enter the heavenly temple (and so try to change God's mind) until the full series of seven plagues might be carried out.

For Reflection: From the perspective of the original readers of Revelation (and from our perspective also) the events to be described in chapter 16 are still future. But in chapter 15 the final victory is celebrated by way of anticipation. On what grounds could this be done? What made John so certain? Where does Jesus' resurrection fit in this schema?

The Seven Bowls (16:1-21)

¹ I heard a loud voice speaking from the temple to the seven angels, "Go and pour out the seven bowls of God's fury upon the earth."

² The first angel went and poured out his bowl on the earth. Festering and ugly sores broke out on those who had the mark of the beast or worshiped its image.

³ The second angel poured out his bowl on the sea. The sea turned to blood like that from a corpse; every creature living in the sea died.

⁴ The third angel poured out his bowl on the rivers and springs of water. These also turned to blood. ⁵ Then I heard the angel in charge of the waters say:
"You are just, O Holy One,
    who are and who were,
    in passing this sentence.
⁶ For they have shed the blood of the holy ones and the prophets,
    and you [have] given them blood to drink;
    it is what they deserve."
⁷ Then I heard the altar cry out,
"Yes, Lord God almighty,
    your judgments are true and just."

⁸ The fourth angel poured out his bowl on the sun. It was given the power to burn people with fire. ⁹ People were burned by the scorching heat and blasphemed the name of God who had power over these plagues, but they did not repent or give him glory.

¹⁰ The fifth angel poured out his bowl on the throne of the beast. Its kingdom was plunged into darkness, and people bit their tongues in pain ¹¹ and blasphemed the God of heaven because of their pains and sores. But they did not repent of their works.

¹² The sixth angel emptied his bowl on the great river Euphrates. Its water was dried up to prepare the way for the kings of the East. ¹³ I saw three unclean spirits like frogs come from the mouth of the dragon, from the mouth of the beast, and from the mouth of the false prophet. ¹⁴ These were demonic spirits who performed signs. They went out to the kings of the whole world to assemble them for the battle on the great day of God the almighty. ¹⁵ ("Behold, I am coming like a thief." Blessed is the one who watches and keeps his clothes ready, so that he may not go naked and people see him exposed.) ¹⁶ They then assembled the kings in the place that is named Armageddon in Hebrew.

¹⁷ The seventh angel poured out his bowl into the air. A loud voice came out of the temple from the throne, saying, "It is done." ¹⁸ Then there were lightning flashes, rumblings, and peals of thunder, and a great earthquake. It was such a violent earthquake that there has never been one like it since the human race began on earth. ¹⁹ The great city was split into three parts, and the gentile cities fell. But God remembered great Babylon, giving it the cup filled with the wine of his fury and wrath. ²⁰ Every island fled, and mountains disappeared. ²¹ Large hailstones like huge weights came down from the sky on people, and they blasphemed God for the plague of hail because this plague was so severe.

The seven bowls in 16:1-21, like the seven seals and the seven trumpets, bring about a series of disasters, evoking again the plagues visited upon Egypt during the exodus (see Ex 7–12). The "loud voice" commanding the seven angels from the heavenly temple (16:1) belongs most likely to God. The bowls contain the various manifestations of God's wrath to be visited upon the earth.

The first bowl (16:2) is poured out on the earth and results in "festering and ugly sores"—as in the sixth plague upon the Egyptians (see Ex 9:10-11; Dt 28:35). The ones who suffer the sores are those who have engaged in worship of the emperor—"those who had the mark of the beast" (see 13:15-16) or "worshiped its image" (see 14:11).

With the second and third bowls (16:3-4) various bodies of water—the sea (16:3), and rivers and springs (16:4)—are turned to blood, just as the Nile River was turned to blood in the exodus (see Ex 7:17-21). The series is interrupted in 16:5-7 by a theological interpretation from the angel in charge of the waters. In 16:5-6 the angel celebrates the justice of God. The "Holy One," who is the eternal one ("who are and who were," see 1:4), is just in punishing those who shed the blood of the "holy ones" (the Christian martyrs) and the prophets (the Old Testament prophets, see Mt 23:37; Lk 13:34-35). It is appropriate that those who shed innocent blood should be forced to drink blood from such rivers and springs. The angel's assessment is confirmed by the altar (16:7), which declares that God's judgments are "true and just."

The fourth bowl (16:8-9) is poured out on the sun, and results in people being burned. And yet they still refuse to repent (see 9:20-21) and instead blaspheme God rather than giving glory to God. This suggests that the ultimate purpose of the plagues associated with the bowls is to bring humans to repentance. That purpose is not fulfilled because of human obduracy, and not because of God's desire to bring harm to humans.

The fifth bowl (16:10-11) is directed toward the "throne of the beast"—the city of Rome or the Roman empire in general. The resulting darkness evokes the plague of darkness upon Egypt (see Ex 10:22). As with the fourth plague, the goal of repentance is not reached. Instead there is even more blasphemy.

The sixth bowl (16:12-16) makes it possible for the "kings of the East" (the Parthians/Persians) to cross the Euphrates River. Here they seem to function more as the allies of Rome than as its enemies. Behind these armies are the "unholy trinity" consisting of the dragon (Satan), the beast (the Roman emperor), and the false prophet (the local official who was persecuting the Christians). The expression "three unclean spirits like frogs" evokes the plague of frogs upon Egypt (see Ex 7:26–8:11). The task of the unclean spirits is to assemble the kings of the earth for the decisive battle "on the great day of God the almighty" (16:14). The parenthetical comment in 16:15 provides assurance and hope to the readers. The coming of Christ will be sudden, but its precise time is not known. Thus he can be said to come "like a thief." The beatitude praises the faithful servant who is always on guard (see Mt 24:36–25:13) and so will not be put to shame ("naked") on the "great day" of the Lord.

According to 16:16 the kings are to assemble at "Armageddon"—the place where the forces of evil are to be defeated by the Lamb. The name "Armageddon" may refer to the "mountain of Megiddo," which was a place of decisive battles in ancient Israel's history (see Jgs 5:19-20; 2 Kgs 23:29-30; 2 Chr 35:20-24). Or it may refer to Jerusalem as the place of the final battle (see Zec 14).

That the seventh bowl (16:17-21) is the last in the series is signified by the heavenly voice that says, "It is done." The seventh bowl brings cosmic portents (16:18), especially the greatest earthquake that the world has ever experienced. The "great city" of 16:19 may be Jerusalem, since "great Babylon" is surely Rome. If so, then this might support identifying Armageddon as Jerusalem in 16:16. For Babylon as drinking the cup of God's wrath, see 14:8-10. No part of the earth—not even islands or mountains—will escape the effects of the seventh bowl. The over one-hundred pound hailstones raining down on the earth evoke the plague of hail upon Egypt in the exodus (see Ex 9:24). As with the fourth and fifth bowls, the result is failure to repent (see 16:9, 11) and further obduracy on the part of those being punished for their sins.

For Reflection: Chapters 15 and 16 offer ample scope for the application of the senses and the imagination. One can hear the song of Moses and of the Lamb (15:3-4), and the proclamation of the angel (16:5-6) and of the altar (16:7). One can smell the "smoke from God's glory" (15:8). One can feel the "festering and ugly sores" (16:2), the burning sun (16:8-9), and the shaking caused by the great earthquake (16:17-21). Above all, one can see the waters turned into blood (16:3-4), the darkness falling on the Roman empire (16:10), the armies massed for battle (16:12), and the damage done by the great earthquake (16:17-21). Like the seven seals and the seven trumpets, the seven bowls affirm the lordship of God and of the Lamb over all human rulers (especially over the Roman emperor and his officials). The series of disasters is apparently intended to lead people to repent and to recognize God as the Lord of all. Instead, human obduracy increases. Why is that so? Why do people refuse to acknowledge God?

XII
The Fall of Babylon/Rome

The occasion for the composition of the book of Revelation was to a large extent the persecution of Christians in western Asia Minor. By refusing to worship the emperor as divine and the goddess Roma as the symbol of the empire, these Christians found themselves in conflict with the local political and religious leaders. Throughout the book, there have been many indications—some subtle, and others quite clear—that John expected God to intervene and bring the Roman empire to an end. These hopes on John's part receive full expression in 17:1–19:10. First there is a vision of Rome as a prostitute (17:1-6) and an interpretation of the vision (17:7-18). Then there are proclamations of Rome's fall by the two angelic voices (18:1-8), by Rome's former clients (18:9-20), and by another angel (18:21-24). The fall of Rome is greeted in 19:1-10 by a series of heavenly songs that feature the term "Alleluia" ("Praise God").

The Vision (17:1-6)

¹ Then one of the seven angels who were holding the seven bowls came and said to me, "Come here. I will show you the judgment on the great harlot who lives near the many waters. ² The kings of the earth have had intercourse with her, and the inhabitants of the earth

became drunk on the wine of her harlotry." [3] Then he carried me away in spirit to a deserted place where I saw a woman seated on a scarlet beast that was covered with blasphemous names, with seven heads and ten horns. [4] The woman was wearing purple and scarlet and was adorned with gold, precious stones, and pearls. She held in her hand a gold cup that was filled with abominable and sordid deeds of her harlotry. [5] On her forehead was written a name, which is a mystery, "Babylon the great, the mother of harlots and of the abominations of the earth." [6] I saw that the woman was drunk on the blood of the holy ones and on the blood of the witnesses to Jesus. When I saw her I was greatly amazed.

The vision is introduced in 17:1-3a. One of the angels in charge of the bowls will serve as the seer's guide in showing him the vision (17:3b-6) and in giving the interpretation (17:7-18). He tells John that the vision concerns "the judgment on the great harlot" (17:1), who is Rome. As the imperial capital, Rome controlled the sea trade on the Mediterranean Sea ("the many waters"). He says that Rome's clients have been corrupted—a corruption described with images of fornication (usually in Revelation a symbol for idolatry, but perhaps here including sexual excesses) and drunkenness (17:2). The angel brings John into the wilderness (17:3a). There may be a contrast here with the vision of the heavenly Jerusalem, which according to 21:10 takes place on "a great high mountain."

The vision (17:3b-6) concerns Rome. The woman adorned as a prostitute is a parody on the goddess Roma as the personification of Rome. The beast would seem to be the Roman emperor (or a series of Roman emperors). The "blasphemous names" (17:4) on the scarlet beast are presumably the pretentious titles given to the emperors ("divine," "lord," august," and so forth). The "seven heads and ten horns" are explained below in the interpretation (see 17:9, 12).

The woman is described in vivid detail in 17:4-6. Her clothing and jewelry are splendid but garish, and her gold cup is full of immoral foulness (17:4). In 17:5 there may be an allusion to Roman prostitutes, who put their names on headbands. The name of this prostitute is "Babylon"—the code-name ("a mystery") for Rome. Whatever terrible things are said about Babylon in the Old Testament can now be transferred to Rome. Here she is described as the root of all the evils in the world ("the mother of harlots and of the abominations of the earth"). In particular, according to 17:6, Rome has been responsible for putting faithful Christians to death. With a gruesome image, Rome is described as drinking the blood of the "holy ones" and the "witnesses to Jesus" to the point of intoxication.

The Interpretation of the Vision (17:7-18)

[7] The angel said to me, "Why are you amazed? I will explain to you the mystery of the woman and of the beast that carries her, the beast with the seven heads and the ten horns. [8] The beast that you saw existed once but now exists no longer. It will come up from the abyss and is headed for destruction. The inhabitants of the earth whose names have not been written in the book of life from the foundation of the world shall be amazed when they see the beast, because it existed once but exists no longer, and yet it will come again. [9] Here is a clue for one who has wisdom. The seven heads represent seven hills upon which the woman sits. They also represent seven kings: [10] five have already fallen, one still

lives, and the last has not yet come, and when he comes he must remain only a short while. [11] The beast that existed once but exists no longer is an eighth king, but really belongs to the seven and is headed for destruction. [12] The ten horns that you saw represent ten kings who have not yet been crowned; they will receive royal authority along with the beast for one hour. [13] They are of one mind and will give their power and authority to the beast. [14] They will fight with the Lamb, but the Lamb will conquer them, for he is Lord of lords and king of kings, and those with him are called, chosen, and faithful."

[15] Then he said to me, "The waters that you saw where the harlot lives represent large numbers of peoples, nations, and tongues. [16] The ten horns that you saw and the beast will hate the harlot; they will leave her desolate and naked; they will eat her flesh and consume her with fire. [17] For God has put it into their minds to carry out his purpose and to make them come to an agreement to give their kingdom to the beast until the words of God are accomplished. [18] The woman whom you saw represents the great city that has sovereignty over the kings of the earth."

Recognizing John's amazement (17:6b), the angel offers to serve as the interpreter of the vision—a common angelic role in Jewish apocalyptic literature. His interpretation deals in turn with the beast (17:8), the seven heads (17:9-11), the ten horns (17:12-14), the waters (17:15-17), and the woman (17:18).

The description of the beast in 17:8 plays on rumors that the emperor Nero had not died in A.D. 68 but rather would return at the head of the Parthian (Persian) army to take revenge on his rivals and enemies. There may be a subtle contrast between the risen Christ (who died and returned to life) and Nero the Antichrist (whose rumored return terrified the Roman leaders).

The seven heads (17:9-11) receive two interpretations. The first interpretation identifies the seven heads with the "seven hills"—an obvious reference to Rome, which was frequently called the "city of seven hills." The second interpretation equates the seven heads with seven Roman emperors. The first five are probably Augustus, Tiberius, Gaius Caligula, Claudius, and Nero. The "one who still lives" may be Vespasian, and "the last" may be his son Titus. The eighth (17:11) would then be Domitian, who reigned from A.D. 81 to 96—in the latter part of whose reign the book of Revelation reached its final form. There were apparently Nero-pretenders emerging from time to time. There is the suggestion that Nero (the first great persecutor of Christians at Rome) and Domitian (in whose empire the Christens of western Asia Minor were being persecuted) were somehow the same.

The ten horns (17:12-14) are said to represent "ten kings" who will ally themselves briefly with the beast. In the light of Nero "restored to life" (*redivivus*) rumors, the ten kings are probably to be understood as the Parthian rulers who were expected to join Nero in trying to place him back on the imperial throne. The Parthians, of course, were the traditional enemies of Rome. The prospect of their alliance with Nero seems based on the principle "the enemy of my enemy is my friend." At any rate, this alliance will be brief and unsuccessful, since "the Lamb will conquer them" (17:14). The Lamb is the risen Christ who is "Lord of lords and King of kings." His companions are "called, chosen, and faithful"—the ideal of Christian life.

See the description of the practically effortless victory of the Lamb in the final battle (19:19-21).

The waters (17:15-17) represent the inhabitants of the Roman empire. They will witness the alliance of Nero (the beast) and the Parthians (the ten horns) as they succeed in inflicting defeat on the woman (Rome). Despite appearances, however, God remains sovereign over all these figures and allows them to destroy each other to achieve his own purposes in fulfilling the promises to God's people ("until the words of God are accomplished").

The woman (17:18), who was the main subject of the vision, is finally identified as "the great city that has sovereignty over the kings of the earth"—a clear reference to Rome.

For Reflection: Although the vision and its interpretation in Revelation 17 contain many obscure elements, there is no doubt about its main point: the expectation that the great enemy of God's people—the Roman empire—will be destroyed soon by God's power and the agency of the Lamb. This would have been dangerous talk in western Asia Minor in the last years of Domitian's reign (A.D. 95-96). It was probably the reason why John was on Patmos. And yet there is no call for a human-led revolution. The victory here belongs to God and the Lamb, and they will bring it about in the appropriate time and way. What theological beliefs led early Christians like John to such a view? Do you share these beliefs?

The Fall of Babylon/Rome (18:1-8)

¹ After this I saw another angel coming down from heaven, having great authority, and the earth became il-

luminated by his splendor. ² He cried out in a mighty
voice:

"Fallen, fallen is Babylon the great.
She has become a haunt for demons.
She is a cage for every unclean spirit,
a cage for every unclean bird,
[a cage for every unclean] and disgusting [beast].
³ For all the nations have drunk
the wine of her licentious passion.
The kings of the earth had intercourse with her,
and the merchants of the earth grew rich from her
drive for luxury."
⁴ Then I heard another voice from heaven say:
"Depart from her, my people,
so as not to take part in her sins
and receive a share in her plagues,
⁵ for her sins are piled up to the sky,
and God remembers her crimes.
⁶ Pay her back as she has paid others.
Pay her back double for her deeds.
Into her cup pour double what she poured.
⁷ To the measure of her boasting and wantonness
repay her in torment and grief;
for she said to herself,
'I sit enthroned as queen;
I am no widow,
and I will never know grief.'
⁸ Therefore her plagues will come in one day,
pestilence, grief, and famine;
she will be consumed by fire.
For mighty is the Lord God who judges her."

The voice of the first angel (18:1-3) proclaims the fall of
Babylon/Rome as if it had already taken place. Of course,
from the perspectives of John and his original audience
this event was still future. But given their faith in God and

the Lamb, it was for them already as good as done. This angel is not the angel of chapter 17 but rather "another" one. His splendor is described in terms used for the glory of God in Ezekiel 43:2. His cry in 18:2 ("Fallen, fallen is Babylon the great") already appeared in 14:8 (see Is 21:9). The descriptions of what had become of Babylon and will become of Rome ("a haunt of demons . . . a cage for every unclean spirit . . . for every unclean bird . . . disgusting beast") echo various biblical texts (Is 13:21-22; Jer 51:31; Is 34:11-15; Jer 50:39). The first two reasons why Babylon/Rome must fall according to 18:3 are familiar: It has corrupted the world by its "licentious passion" (immoral behavior?) and by fornication (idolatry?). But 18:3 adds a new reason—economic exploitation and greed, which is developed at some length in 18:9-20.

The second voice ("another voice from heaven") that speaks in 18:4-8 is probably that of an angel rather than that of God or the Lamb. The first part of his proclamation (18:4-5) is directed to "my people" and tells them to have nothing to do with the Roman empire, lest they share also in the punishment for its sins. The language echoes Jeremiah's words about Babylon in the sixth century B.C. (see Jer 51:45; 50:8; etc.).

The second part (18:6-8) presents a serious problem. If addressed to "my people" (as in 18:4), this would be the only part of Revelation that suggests that Christians take an active role in punishing the Roman empire for its sins. Everything else in the book attributes that task to God, the Lamb, the angels, and nature. Therefore perhaps 18:6-8 should be taken as spoken to other angels ("pay her back . . . repay her"; see 18:20 where there is a sudden change of address) or to Nero "restored to life" (*redivivus*)

135

and his Parthian allies. The second angel urges them to re-pay Babylon/Rome double for its sins of pride and corrupt behavior. In 18:7b, the female personification of Rome (Roma) imagines that nothing can change her status as the world sovereign ("queen . . . no widow"). The disasters that will come upon her suddenly ("in one day") and deci-sively ("consumed by fire") will show all the world who re-ally is the sovereign lord ("mighty is the Lord God who judges her").

The Kings', Merchants', and Sailors' Lament (18:9-20)

⁹ The kings of the earth who had intercourse with her in their wantonness will weep and mourn over her when they see the smoke of her pyre. ¹⁰ They will keep their distance for fear of the torment inflicted on her, and they will say:
"Alas, alas, great city,
    Babylon, mighty city.
    In one hour your judgment has come."
¹¹ The merchants of the earth will weep and mourn for her, because there will be no more markets for their cargo: ¹² their cargo of gold, silver, precious stones, and pearls; fine linen, purple silk, and scarlet cloth; fragrant wood of every kind, all articles of ivory and all articles of the most expensive wood, bronze, iron, and marble; ¹³ cinnamon, spice, incense, myrrh, and frankincense; wine, olive oil, fine flour, and wheat; cattle and sheep, horses and chariots, and slaves, that is, human beings.
¹⁴ "The fruit you craved
        has left you.
    All your luxury and splendor are gone,
        never again will one find them."
¹⁵ The merchants who deal in these goods, who grew rich from her, will keep their distance for fear of the tor-

ment inflicted on her. Weeping and mourning, [16] they
cry out:

"Alas, alas, great city,
    wearing fine linen, purple and scarlet,
    adorned [in] gold, precious stones, and pearls.
[17] In one hour this great wealth has been ruined."

Every captain of a ship, every traveler at sea, sailors
and seafaring merchants stood at a distance [18] and cried
out when they saw the smoke of her pyre, "What city
could compare with the great city?" [19] They threw dust
on their heads and cried out, weeping and mourning:

"Alas, alas, great city,
    in which all who had ships at sea
    grew rich from her wealth.
    In one hour she has been ruined."
[20] "Rejoice over her, heaven,
    you holy ones, apostles, and prophets.
    For God has judged your case against her."

The angelic proclamation of Babylon/Rome's fall in
18:1-8 is supplemented by the dirges sung over Rome by
its former clients: the kings of the earth (18:9-10), the
merchants of the earth (18:11-17a), and the sailors who
transported Rome's goods (18:17b-19). They all use the
language of the lament over Tyre in Ezekiel 26–27.

The client kings (18:9-10), who once eagerly joined in
Rome's social and religious aggression ("had intercourse
with her in their wantonness"), now keep their distance
and adopt the role of observers: "Alas, alas, great city."
They lament how quickly Babylon/Rome's fall took place
(or, will take place)—"in one hour."

The second group (18:11-17a) consists of "merchants
of the earth" who profited from doing business with
Rome. Their business ventures are now frustrated, because Rome is (or, will be) no more. The list of goods that

these merchants traded (18:12-13), while based on Ezekiel 27:12-24, gives precious insight into the economic dimensions of the Roman empire. As the imperial capital, Rome drew to itself the luxury goods of its clients. The list ends on a chilling but realistic note ("and slaves, that is, human beings").

The first part of the merchants' lament (18:14) bewails the fact that Rome will no more enjoy its status as the city to which all luxury goods naturally flowed. The second part (18:15-17a) echoes the lament of the client kings. The merchants too "keep their distance" and adopt the stance of observers rather than participants. They too raise a lament over Rome ("alas, alas, great city") and comment on the suddenness of the fall ("in one hour"). Since their interests are economic and their focus is their own business interests, the merchants mourn the passing of their opportunities to trade in luxury goods.

The sailors (18:17b-19) echo the sentiments of the preceding groups. They too adopt the posture of observers, lament the fall of Babylon/Rome ("alas, alas, great city"), and note how suddenly it took (or, will take) place. The passage also gives further insight into how the economy of the Roman empire worked. The luxury goods from the far reaches of the empire were conveyed by ships all over the Mediterranean Sea: "All who had ships at sea grew rich from her wealth." Again the lament of these people is a mixture of sympathy for the lost glory of Rome ("What city could compare with the great city?") and self-interested concern for their own loss of business opportunities.

The comment in 18:20 is probably not part of the merchants' lament but rather is from John or from an angel. It urges the angels of heaven and the faithful Christians to rejoice over the fall of Rome and to interpret it as a divine judgment and a vindication of God's faithful witnesses.

Another Lament (18:21-24)

²¹ A mighty angel picked up a stone like a huge millstone and threw it into the sea and said:
"With such force will Babylon the great city be thrown down,
and will never be found again.
²² No melodies of harpists and musicians,
flutists and trumpeters,
will ever be heard in you again.
No craftsman in any trade
will ever be found in you again.
No sound of the millstone
will ever be heard in you again.
²³ No light from a lamp
will ever be seen in you again.
No voices of bride and groom
will ever be heard in you again.
Because your merchants were the great ones of the world,
all nations were led astray by your magic potion.
²⁴ In her was found the blood of prophets and holy ones
and all who have been slain on the earth."

As the first lament over Babylon/Rome (18:1-8) came from an angel, so does the third lament (18:21-24). By throwing a huge stone into the sea as a symbolic representation of Rome's fall, the angel does what the reader of Jeremiah's prophecies against Babylon was told to do (see Jer 51:63-64). The angel's lament (18:21b-24) first establishes the utter destruction (to be) visited upon Babylon/Rome: "and will never be found again" (18:21b). The images in 18:22-23a evoke scenes of a peaceful and contented and well-ordered society—with pleasant music, artisans at work, light in darkness, and weddings—that is (or, will be) no more. According to 18:23b-24 there are two reasons for the fall of Babylon/Rome: Its merchants corrupted all the nations (18:23b), and it persecuted and killed God's faithful witnesses ("the blood of the prophets and holy ones," 18:24).

For Reflection: As in chapter 17, so in chapter 18 the future fall of Rome is presented as having already taken place. And again what was to happen to Babylon according to the Old Testament prophets was to happen to Rome as the oppressor of God's people. What is especially interesting in chapter 18 is the portrait of the dynamics between the imperial city of Rome and its client rulers and merchants. We see vividly the economic conditions that prevailed in the Roman empire while it flourished. We also see the fickleness and self-centeredness of Rome's clients after its fall. Can you think of analogies in the nineteenth and twentieth centuries? What reasons does chapter 18 give for Rome's fall? Which ones do you regard as most important?

The Victory Liturgy (19:1-10)

> [1] After this I heard what sounded like the loud voice of a great multitude in heaven, saying:
> "Alleluia!
> Salvation, glory, and might belong to our God,
> [2] for true and just are his judgments.
> He has condemned the great harlot

who corrupted the earth with her harlotry.
He has avenged on her the blood of his servants."
³ They said a second time:
"Alleluia! Smoke will rise from her forever and ever."
⁴ The twenty-four elders and the four living creatures
fell down and worshiped God who sat on the throne,
saying, "Amen. Alleluia."
⁵ A voice coming from the throne said:
"Praise our God, all you his servants,
[and] you who revere him, small and great."
⁶ Then I heard something like the sound of a great
multitude or the sound of rushing water or mighty peals
of thunder, as they said: "Alleluia!
The Lord has established his reign,
[our] God, the almighty.
⁷ Let us rejoice and be glad
and give him glory.
For the wedding day of the Lamb has come,
his bride has made herself ready.
⁸ She was allowed to wear
a bright, clean linen garment."
(The linen represents the righteous deeds of the
holy ones.)
⁹ Then the angel said to me, "Write this: Blessed are
those who have been called to the wedding feast of the
Lamb." And he said to me, "These words are true; they
come from God." ¹⁰ I fell at his feet to worship him. But
he said to me, "Don't! I am a fellow servant of yours and
of your brothers who bear witness to Jesus. Worship
God. Witness to Jesus is the spirit of prophecy."

As a complement to the laments over Rome's fall ut-
tered by angels and humans in chapter 18, the first part of
chapter 19 (vv. 1-8) is a victory liturgy with songs that feature the Hebrew word "Alleluia" ("praise God") and express the triumph of God and the Lamb over the Roman

empire. These songs also prepare for the final and full manifestation of God's kingdom that is to be described in 19:11–22:5. The victory songs come from the "great multitude" (19:1b-2, 3), the elders and the four living creatures (19:4), the voice coming from the throne (19:5), and again a "great multitude" (19:6-8). An interchange between the angel and John rounds off the passage (19:9-10).

The "great multitude in heaven" (19:1a) consists more likely of angels than of the Christian martyrs. Their first song (19:1b-2) interprets the fall of Rome as a proof of God's justice; it is punishment for Rome's sins, and especially for putting God's servants to death. Their second song (19:3) stresses the definitive character of Rome's defeat: "Smoke will rise from her forever and ever."

The members of the inner circle in the heavenly court—the twenty-four elders and the four living creatures (see 4:1-11)—in 19:4 affirm the angelic song by saying, "Amen. Alleluia." "Amen" means "I believe that it is so," and "Alleluia" means "Praise God."

The voice coming from the throne (19:5) is more likely that of one of the elders or living creatures than that of God (who is praised) or of the Lamb. Their song is the equivalent of "Alleluia"—a call to praise God.

The final song (19:6-8) comes from the entire heavenly host. It first celebrates the establishment of God's kingdom in its fullness (19:6b-7a). Then in 19:7b-8 it describes this event as the wedding feast of the Lamb. The imagery is based on various Old Testament passages (see Hos 2:16-22; Is 54:5-6; 62:5; Ez 16:6-14) that depict God's relationship with Israel in terms of a marriage. Likewise, idolatry can be described as fornication and prostitution (see Hos 2:4-15; Ez 16:15-63). Here the bride of the Lamb is the people of God, which in Revelation is the Church. In contrast to ancient Israel, the Church is a faithful bride. And in contrast to the prostitute Roma (who dresses garishly; see 17:1-6), the Church-bride wears a "bright, clean linen garment"—symbolic both of her moral purity and of her fidelity in facing martyrdom (see 7:13-17). The parenthetical comment in 19:8b equates the linen garment with the righteous deeds of the faithful.

The interchange between the angel and John in 19:9-10 (see also 22:8-9) functions as an interlude. In 19:9 the angel instructs the seer to write down another beatitude (the fourth of seven) about those who are called to the Lamb's wedding feast and an affirmation that God's promises are true. In 19:10 John's confused attempt to worship the angel serves to highlight the difference between angels and humans (however glorious) on the one hand and God and the risen Jesus on the other hand. The parenthetical comment at the end of 19:10 ("witness to Jesus is the spirit of prophecy") links the divine inspiration behind the biblical prophets and that behind the Christian martyrs.

For Reflection: The victory liturgy in 19:1-10 takes readers into the heavenly court and invites them to join the heavenly chorus in praising God. It celebrates the omnipotence of God (the "almighty," 19:6) and the justice of God ("true and just are his judgments," 19:2). It also paints a beautiful picture of the relationship between Christ and the Church in terms of bride and groom. These texts (and many more) in Revelation have influenced Christian hymnody for centuries (for example, "Holy

God, We Praise Thy Name"). Are you able to make these songs your own? Why? Why not?

XIII

The Last Apocalyptic Scenario

Thus far the book of Revelation has featured several series of end-time events: seven seals, seven trumpets, and seven bowls. As the book nears its close, one more apocalyptic scenario portrays the definitive defeat of evil and the absolute triumph of God, the Lamb, and the faithful witnesses. Again there are many similarities with the "little apocalypse" presented in Mark 13, Matthew 24–25, and Luke 21. The most distinctive features are the risen Christ/Lamb as a warrior, the binding of Satan and his subsequent short-term release, and the thousand-year reign of Christ and the righteous (the millennium).

The last apocalyptic scenario proceeds in seven steps or phases: the parousia (19:11-16), the first battle (19:17-21), the binding of Satan (20:1-3), the first resurrection (20:4-6), the final defeat of Satan in the last battle (20:7-10), the last judgment (20:11-15), and the new heaven and the new earth (21:1-8).

The Parousia (19:11-16)

[11] Then I saw the heavens opened, and there was a white horse; its rider was [called] "Faithful and True." He judges and wages war in righteousness. [12] His eyes were [like] a fiery flame, and on his head were many diadems. He had a name inscribed that no one knows ex-

cept himself. [13] He wore a cloak that had been dipped in blood, and his name was called the Word of God. [14] The armies of heaven followed him, mounted on white horses and wearing clean white linen. [15] Out of his mouth came a sharp sword to strike the nations. He will rule them with an iron rod, and he himself will tread out in the wine press the wine of the fury and wrath of God the almighty. [16] He has a name written on his cloak and on his thigh, "King of kings and Lord of lords."

The initial phase (19:11-16) consists of the appearance or presence (parousia) of the risen Christ as a mighty warrior. When heaven opens up, John sees the white horse and its rider. The description of the rider as "Faithful and True" (19:11) serves to identify him as the risen Christ (see 1:5; 3:7) and the purpose of his activities as an instrument of God's justice. In 19:12 he is further described as having eyes like a fiery flame (see 1:4). The fact that he has "many diadems" indicates his sovereignty over many nations, not just one or two. The name known to him alone may reflect the idea that knowing someone's name gives one power over that person. No one has power over the risen Christ. Or perhaps that name is revealed immediately as "Word of God" (19:13) or "King of kings and Lord of lords" (19:16). The cloak "dipped in blood" refers to the divine warrior figure in Isaiah 63:1-3 (see Rv 14:17-20) as well as to the blood shed by the Lamb that was slain. The title "Word of God," so familiar from John 1:1, here evokes the description of Wisdom as a warrior in the book of Wisdom 18:15: "Your all-powerful word from heaven's royal throne bounded, a fierce warrior, into the doomed land."

Accompanied by the armies of heaven (19:14), who join him in battle, the divine warrior/risen Christ acts as the Messiah of the scriptures by striking the nations with the sword coming from his mouth (see Is 11:4), by ruling them with an iron rod (see Ps 2:9), and treading the winepress of God's wrath (see Is 63:3). The name written on his cloak and thigh—"King of kings and Lord of lords" (19:16)—establishes the risen Christ as superior to any human ruler, even and especially the Roman emperor. In the battle that follows he shows himself master of the beast and the kings of the earth as well as the false prophet.

For Reflection: Many striking images are applied here to the risen Christ. Which impress you most—positively and negatively? How do you react to the depiction of Christ as a warrior?

The First Battle (19:17-21)

17 Then I saw an angel standing on the sun. He cried out [in] a loud voice to all the birds flying high overhead, "Come here. Gather for God's great feast, 18 to eat the flesh of kings, the flesh of military officers, and the flesh of warriors, the flesh of horses and of their riders, and the flesh of all, free and slave, small and great." 19 Then I saw the beast and the kings of the earth and their armies gathered to fight against the one riding the horse and against his army. 20 The beast was caught and with it the false prophet who had performed in its sight the signs by which he led astray those who had accepted the mark of the beast and those who had worshiped its image. The two were thrown alive into the fiery pool burning with sulfur. 21 The rest were killed by the sword

147

that came out of the mouth of the one riding the horse, and all the birds gorged themselves on their flesh.

The second phase (19:17-21) is the battle. And yet so powerful is the divine warrior/risen Christ that there is hardly a battle at all. In 19:17-18 an angel summons the birds of prey (such as vultures) to prepare for "God's great feast"—a feast provided by God (see Ez 39:17-20). The feast will consist of human flesh from all ranks—from kings and officers to "free and slave, small and great." The forces arrayed against the divine warrior/risen Christ consist of the beast (the Roman emperor) and the kings of the earth (19:19).

The battle itself is described in only two verses (19:20-21). The divine warrior/risen Christ defeats not only the beast but also the false prophet (the local official in western Asia Minor, who promoted worship of the emperor and Roma, and who was responsible for persecuting the Christians to whom John wrote). The description of the false prophet here recalls what was said about him in 13:11-17. The beast and the false prophet are thrown into "the fiery pool burning with sulfur" (see 14:10; 20:10, 14-15). They receive special (negative) treatment, a fitting punishment for their special hostility to the people of God. The rest are easily defeated by the Word of God (see 19:13, 15) and become food for the birds (see 19:17-18).

For Reflection: The great battle to which the whole book thus far has been pointing is really no contest at all. The Word of God simply overwhelms the beast, the false prophet, and their associates. In fact, the battle against the forces of evil was already won with Jesus' resurrection.

148

Does this text reflect a vengeful attitude? Or does it convey a hopeful attitude?

The Binding of Satan (20:1-3)

> [1] Then I saw an angel come down from heaven, holding in his hand the key to the abyss and a heavy chain. [2] He seized the dragon, the ancient serpent, which is the Devil or Satan, and tied it up for a thousand years [3] and threw it into the abyss, which he locked over it and sealed, so that it could no longer lead the nations astray until the thousand years are completed. After this, it is to be released for a short time.

The third phase (20:1-3) is the binding of Satan, who is the power behind the beast and the false prophet in their unholy trinity. The "abyss" (20:1) to which Satan is consigned is a temporary holding place, not his final destination (see 20:10). The "heavy chain" is to keep Satan bound up. The "dragon" (20:2) has been previously identified as the ancient serpent, the Devil, and Satan (see 12:9). His binding is to last for a thousand years (the millennium). During that time, Satan will not be able to "lead the nations astray" (20:3). After the millennium, God will allow Satan to be set free for a short time, until his ultimate punishment (see 20:10).

For Reflection: During the millennium Satan cannot exercise power over humans, and so God's will can be done on earth as it is done in heaven. Can you imagine a world without sin and evil? Why will God let Satan loose again, even if for only a short while?

The First Resurrection (20:4-6)

⁴ Then I saw thrones; those who sat on them were entrusted with judgment. I also saw the souls of those who had been beheaded for their witness to Jesus and for the word of God, and who had not worshiped the beast or its image nor had accepted its mark on their foreheads or hands. They came to life and they reigned with Christ for a thousand years. ⁵ The rest of the dead did not come to life until the thousand years were over. This is the first resurrection. ⁶ Blessed and holy is the one who shares in the first resurrection. The second death has no power over these; they will be priests of God and of Christ, and they will reign with him for [the] thousand years.

The fourth phase (20:4-6) is the "first resurrection"—the restoration to life of those who had remained faithful even to the point of death. These are described in 20:4 with terms already used for the martyrs in 13:15-16, with particular attention given to their refusal to engage in worshiping the emperor ("who had not worshiped the beast or his image") on religious grounds ("for their witness to Jesus"). Their reward is the "first resurrection," which lasts for a thousand years and precedes the general resurrection. Thus the victorious martyrs share in the Satan-free millennial reign of the risen Christ. With the fifth beatitude (20:6; see 1:3; 14:13; 16:15; 19:9; 22:7, 14) they are declared "blessed." Over them the "second death" (eternal punishment after physical death, see 20:14-15) has no power. Rather, they serve as "priests of God and of Christ" (see 1:6; 5:10), devoting themselves to the worship of God during the millennium.

150

For Reflection: The term "millennium" is used quite concretely in 20:4-6. How does it differ from popular uses of the term today? Who enjoys the millennium here, and why?

The Final Defeat of Satan (20:7-10)

[7] When the thousand years are completed, Satan will be released from his prison. [8] He will go out to deceive the nations at the four corners of the earth, Gog and Magog, to gather them for battle; their number is like the sand of the sea. [9] They invaded the breadth of the earth and surrounded the camp of the holy ones and the beloved city. But fire came down from heaven and consumed them. [10] The Devil who had led them astray was thrown into the pool of fire and sulfur, where the beast and the false prophet were. There they will be tormented day and night forever and ever.

The fifth phase (20:7-10) is the definitive defeat of Satan. After his release from bondage (20:7; see 20:1-3), Satan is to be active again "for a short time" (see 20:3). He will gather nations from all over the world, symbolized as "Gog and Magog" from Ezekiel 38–39, for one last attack upon "the camp of the holy ones and the beloved city" (see 21:10, where such language is used about the new Jerusalem). As in 19:17-21 when the beast and the false prophet were defeated, there is not much of a battle. Rather, it is simply a matter of fire coming down from heaven and destroying these armies (20:9b; see 2 Kgs 1:10; Ez 38:22; 39:6). Now Satan's power is broken completely, and he is consigned to suffer eternal punishment with the other members of the "unholy trinity"—the beast and the false prophet (20:10; see 19:20).

151

For Reflection: In the Lord's Prayer we say, "Deliver us from the evil one" (Mt 6:13). That text also envisions a final period of testing or trial when Satan is especially active. Do you see links in content and imagery between the Lord's Prayer (Mt 6:9-13; Lk 11:2-4) and the book of Revelation?

The Last Judgment (20:11-15)

> [11] Next I saw a large white throne and the one who was sitting on it. The earth and the sky fled from his presence and there was no place for them. [12] I saw the dead, the great and the lowly, standing before the throne, and scrolls were opened. Then another scroll was opened, the book of life. The dead were judged according to their deeds, by what was written in the scrolls. [13] The sea gave up its dead; then Death and Hades gave up their dead. All the dead were judged according to their deeds. [14] Then Death and Hades were thrown into the pool of fire. (This pool of fire is the second death.) [15] Anyone whose name was not found written in the book of life was thrown into the pool of fire.

The sixth phase (20:11-15) concerns the last judgment of those who have died, apart from the martyrs who already enjoy the "first resurrection" (see 20:4-6). The judge here is God (as in Daniel 7), and there is no room for anything else (20:11; see 21:1, where a new heaven and a new earth appear). In 20:12-13 all the dead are restored to some kind of life and are judged "according to their deeds," which are written in the "book of life" (see Dn 7:10). The personifications of death ("Death") and of the abode of the dead ("Hades") not only give up their dead but are also consigned to the pool of fire with Satan, the beast, and the false prophet. They are joined by those whose names are absent from the book of life. This "pool of fire"—the basis of the traditional concept of hell—is equated with the "second death," which consists in separation from God and in eternal punishment.

For Reflection: The last judgment involves the punishment of the enemies of God and God's people. How do you reconcile this with the mercy of God? Can both justice and mercy be attributes of God?

The New Heaven and the New Earth (21:1-8)

¹ Then I saw a new heaven and a new earth. The former heaven and the former earth had passed away, and the sea was no more. ² I also saw the holy city, a new Jerusalem, coming down out of heaven from God, prepared as a bride adorned for her husband. ³ I heard a loud voice from the throne saying, "Behold, God's dwelling is with the human race. He will dwell with them and they will be his people and God himself will always be with them [as their God]. ⁴ He will wipe every tear from their eyes, and there shall be no more death or mourning, wailing or pain, [for] the old order has passed away."

⁵ The one who sat on the throne said, "Behold, I make all things new." Then he said, "Write these words down, for they are trustworthy and true." ⁶ He said to me, "They are accomplished. I [am] the Alpha and the Omega, the beginning and the end. To the thirsty I will give a gift from the spring of life-giving water. ⁷ The victor will inherit these gifts, and I shall be his God, and he will be my son. ⁸ But as for cowards, the unfaithful, the depraved, murderers, the unchaste, sorcerers, idol-worshipers, and deceivers of every sort, their lot is

in the burning pool of fire and sulfur, which is the second death."

The seventh and final phase (21:1-4) brings a new heaven and a new earth. According to 20:11, the old earth and sky had fled from God's presence. The new heaven and new earth replace them (21:1). Moreover, according to 21:2, the new Jerusalem descends from heaven to replace the old one as the special dwelling place of God. For earlier bridal imagery applied to the Church, see 19:7: "For the wedding day of the Lamb has come, his bride has made herself ready." The old separation between heaven and earth is ended, and so God will now dwell with the righteous people of God on earth (21:3). God's will is done on earth as it is in heaven (see Mt 6:10). All suffering and death will be banished, since there will be no more Satan and no more sin. The image of God wiping away tears is based on Isaiah 25:8: "The Lord GOD will wipe away the tears from all faces." The result of this seven-phase eschatological scenario will be perfect peace and happiness between God and all the faithful witnesses to the Lamb and his gospel.

The final scene is supplemented in 21:5-8 with three sayings from God. The first saying ("Behold, I make all things new," 21:5) gives first-person expression to what has already been described in 21:1-4. The second saying (21:5b) is directed to John the seer and confirms his vision-report as "trustworthy and true" (see 19:9). The third saying (21:6-8) is more elaborate. It first (21:6) reuses terms for God ("the Alpha and the Omega") that appeared at the beginning of the book (see 1:8). Then in 21:7 it promises to the "victor" (see the frequent use of this theme in the letters to the seven churches in chapters 2 and 3) the "gifts" described in 21:1-4 and a share in the Father-Son relationship enjoyed by Jesus the Messiah (see 2 Sam 7:14 for the roots of this language). However, the lot of the wicked according to 21:8 is to be with Satan, the beast, and the false prophet in the "burning pool of fire and sulfur, which is the second death."

For Reflection: "Thy will be done on earth as it is in heaven" (Mt 6:10)—the meaning of that prayer can be glimpsed from the picture of the new heaven and the new earth in 21:1-8. How do you imagine eternal life with God?

XIV

The New Jerusalem

This final and climactic scene takes its starting point (21:9-11) from 21:2: "I saw the holy city, a new Jerusalem, coming down out of heaven from God, prepared as a bride adorned for her husband." Then in 21:12-21 there is a description of the new Jerusalem's walls and gates, and its measurements. Finally in 21:22–22:5 we are brought inside the city to see the light and life that reflect the splendor of God and of the Lamb.

The New Jerusalem—An Overview (21:9-21)

[9] One of the seven angels who held the seven bowls filled with the seven last plagues came and said to me, "Come here. I will show you the bride, the wife of the Lamb." [10] He took me in spirit to a great, high mountain and showed me the holy city Jerusalem coming down out of heaven from God. [11] It gleamed with the splendor of God. Its radiance was like that of a precious stone, like jasper, clear as crystal. [12] It had a massive, high wall, with twelve gates where twelve angels were stationed and on which names were inscribed, [the names] of the twelve tribes of the Israelites. [13] There were three gates facing east, three north, three south, and three west. [14] The wall of the city had twelve courses of stones as its foundation, on which were inscribed the twelve names of the twelve apostles of the Lamb.

156

[15] The one who spoke to me held a gold measuring rod to measure the city, its gates, and its wall. [16] The city was square, its length the same as [also] its width. He measured the city with the rod and found it fifteen hundred miles in length and width and height. [17] He also measured its wall: one hundred and forty-four cubits according to the standard unit of measurement the angel used. [18] The wall was constructed of jasper, while the city was pure gold, clear as glass. [19] The foundations of the city wall were decorated with every precious stone; the first course of stones was jasper, the second sapphire, the third chalcedony, the fourth emerald, [20] the fifth sardonyx, the sixth carnelian, the seventh chrysolite, the eighth beryl, the ninth topaz, the tenth chrysoprase, the eleventh hyacinth, and the twelfth amethyst. [21] The twelve gates were twelve pearls, each of the gates made from a single pearl; and the street of the city was of pure gold, transparent as glass.

Just as one of the seven angels who had the seven bowls showed to John the prostitute representing the imperial city of Rome in 17:1-6, so one of these same angels shows him the new Jerusalem as "the bride, the wife of the Lamb" (21:9; see 19:7). This holy city has its origin with God ("coming down out of heaven," 21:10), and it shares the glory of God (which in 21:11 is compared with jasper stone). The new Jerusalem combines the motifs of the restored post-exilic Jerusalem (see Zec 2:1-5; Hag 2:7-9; Is 60:10-14), the restored garden of God or Eden (Gn 2–3), and the heavenly city or city of the gods (in many ancient literatures). The theme of the new (ideal) Jerusalem is developed at even greater length in Ezekiel 40–48 and in the New Jerusalem texts and the *Temple Scroll* among the Dead Sea scrolls.

The description of the new Jerusalem from the outside (21:12-21) gives particular attention to the wall and the twelve gates. Each of the twelve gates (21:12-13) has an angel stationed at it and the name of one of the twelve tribes of Israel inscribed on it. The three gates on each of the four sides of the wall allow entry from any direction. The twelve foundation stones (21:14) bear the names of the twelve apostles, who themselves represent the twelve tribes of Israel (see Mt 19:28). For the decoration of these foundation stones, see 21:19-20.

Meanwhile in 21:15-17 the angel, as in Ezekiel 40–42, sets out to measure the new Jerusalem and its wall and gates. The city forms an enormous cube, about 1,500 miles in length, width, and height, respectively (21:16). The wall around the city, according to 21:17, is about 220 feet high, a huge wall surely but not for a city that is 1,500 miles high.

The material out of which the wall is made (21:18) is precious jasper, and the city itself is translucent gold—both intended to highlight the city's splendor. The list of the precious stones that decorate the foundation stones (21:19-20) is based on the gems that decorated the high priest's breastplate according to Exodus 28:17-20 and 39:10-13 (see also Ez 28:13). Each of the twelve gates is made of a huge pearl, and the street is translucent gold (21:21).

For Reflection: The political theme of the book is carried on in the beginning of 21:9-21 by the implied contrast between the bride/new Jerusalem and the prostitute/Rome of chapters 17 and 18. But this theme yields quickly to the vision of a city of almost unimaginable splendor and size.

158

This is where God and the faithful will dwell. How do you imagine heaven and eternal life with God?

Inside the New Jerusalem (21:22–22:5)

²²I saw no temple in the city, for its temple is the Lord God almighty and the Lamb. ²³ The city had no need of sun or moon to shine on it, for the glory of God gave it light, and its lamp was the Lamb. ²⁴ The nations will walk by its light, and to it the kings of the earth will bring their treasure. ²⁵ During the day its gates will never be shut, and there will be no night there. ²⁶ The treasure and wealth of the nations will be brought there, ²⁷ but nothing unclean will enter it, nor anyone who does abominable things or tells lies. Only those will enter whose names are written in the Lamb's book of life. ²²:¹ Then the angel showed me the river of life-giving water, sparkling like crystal, flowing from the throne of God and of the Lamb ² down the middle of the street. On either side of the river grew the tree of life that produces fruit twelve times a year, once each month; the leaves of the trees serve as medicine for the nations. ³ Nothing accursed will be found there anymore. The throne of God and of the Lamb will be in it, and his servants will worship him. ⁴ They will look upon his face, and his name will be on their foreheads. ⁵ Night will be no more, nor will they need light from lamp or sun, for the Lord God shall give them light, and they shall reign forever and ever.

The new Jerusalem is remarkable for what it does not need. It needs no temple (21:22) because God and the Lamb are there. It needs no lights (21:23) because God's glory gives it light and the Lamb is its lamp (see Is 60:19-20). All the nations will see its light and come to it (21:24; see Is 60:3), and its gates will never be shut

(21:25; see Is 60:11). It will be the destination of the "wealth of the nations" (21:26; see Is 60:5-7). In contrast with Babylon/Rome which was full of abominations (see 17:4), nothing unclean and no one who is abominable shall enter it (21:27; see Is 52:1; 35:8; Ez 44:9).

According to 22:1-2, the new Jerusalem has a "river of life-giving water" (see Gn 2:10) that comes from God and runs down the middle of the street. Here there are two trees of life (see Gn 2:9, where there is only one). The two trees on each side of the river produce fresh fruit every month, and their leaves serve as medicine (see Ez 47:12).

Life within the new Jerusalem (22:3-5) is devoted to the perpetual worship of God. Nothing "accursed" (22:3) can exist alongside the throne of God and of the Lamb (see 21:27; Zec 14:11). God's servants will look upon God's face, and God's name will be on their foreheads (22:4; see 7:3 and 14:1; and by contrast 13:16). Their light will be supplied by the Lord God (see 21:23), and they will share the reign of God and the Lamb.

For Reflection: The new Jerusalem is full of light and life. Worship of God is the one activity that occupies everyone. This is a picture of eternal happiness with God. Our liturgies on earth are at best pale reflections of the liturgy of the new Jerusalem. Nevertheless, they have as their model and ideal the kind of perfect, heavenly worship that is described here. What might such a model mean for the worship conducted in your church or community?

160

XV
Epilogue

Far from being a neat summary of the work as a whole, the final verses (22:6-21) appear to be a collection of disparate sayings, much like the end of the book of Daniel (12:4-13). The ten sayings revolve around three themes: the authenticity of the prophet's message, the imminence of the Lord's coming ("I am coming soon"), and exhortations to the readers/listeners to remain faithful. These are, of course, major themes in the book. And so in that sense 22:6-21 can be said to constitute an epilogue or summary.

Ten Sayings (22:6-21)

6 And he said to me, "These words are trustworthy and true, and the Lord, the God of prophetic spirits, sent his angel to show his servants what must happen soon." 7 "Behold, I am coming soon." Blessed is the one who keeps the prophetic message of this book.

8 It is I, John, who heard and saw these things, and when I heard and saw them I fell down to worship at the feet of the angel who showed them to me. 9 But he said to me, "Don't! I am a fellow servant of yours and of your brothers the prophets and of those who keep the message of this book. Worship God."

10 Then he said to me, "Do not seal up the prophetic words of this book, for the appointed time is near. 11 Let

the wicked still act wickedly, and the filthy still be filthy. The righteous must still do right, and the holy still be holy."

[12] "Behold, I am coming soon. I bring with me the recompense I will give to each according to his deeds. [13] I am the Alpha and the Omega, the first and the last, the beginning and the end."

[14] Blessed are they who wash their robes so as to have the right to the tree of life and enter the city through its gates. [15] Outside are the dogs, the sorcerers, the unchaste, the murderers, the idol-worshipers, and all who love and practice deceit.

[16] "I, Jesus, sent my angel to give you this testimony for the churches. I am the root and offspring of David, the bright morning star."

[17] The Spirit and the bride say, "Come." Let the hearer say, "Come." Let the one who thirsts come forward, and the one who wants it receive the gift of life-giving water.

[18] I warn everyone who hears the prophetic words in this book: If anyone adds to them, God will add to him the plagues described in this book, [19] and if anyone takes away from the words in this prophetic book, God will take away his share in the tree of life and in the holy city described in this book.

[20] The one who gives testimony says, "Yes, I am coming soon." Amen! Come, Lord Jesus!

[21] The grace of the Lord Jesus be with all.

The first saying (22:6-7) comes from the risen Christ who authenticates John's words as "trustworthy and true," proclaims that he will come soon, and uses the sixth of the seven beatitudes to declare "blessed" those who keep the words of the prophecy (see 1:3).

The second saying (22:8-9) is for the most part a report of the encounter between John and the angelic interpreter (see 19:10). The idea of the saying is not to confuse the messenger with the message (which is "worship God").

The third saying (22:10-11) first warns against sealing up (and thus making inaccessible) this prophetic book. Then it suggests that people will act badly or well as they wish. The implication is that the book will help them to know the rewards and punishments for their behaviors, and what is at stake.

The fourth saying (22:12-13) is also from the risen Christ. It repeats the promise that he is coming soon and will bring rewards and punishments to "each according to his deeds." He also takes to himself the titles that earlier (1:8) are attributed to God: "the Alpha and the Omega."

The fifth saying (22:14-15) is a beatitude that contrasts the faithful witnesses who can enter the new Jerusalem and the evildoers who must remain outside.

In the sixth saying (22:16) the risen Christ declares again that he stands behind the book. He then proclaims himself to be the root and offspring of David (see Is 11:1; Rv 5:5) as well as the "bright morning star" (see Nm 24:17 and Rv 2:28)—perhaps the first star or planet (Venus) visible in the morning sky.

The seventh saying (22:17) has the Spirit (the Spirit of Christ) and the bride (the Church) issue an invitation to receive the life-giving waters (see Is 55:1; Jn 7:37).

The eighth saying (22:18-19) is a warning against adding or subtracting from words contained in John's Revelation (see Dt 4:2; 13:1). Such a one cannot expect to enter the new Jerusalem.

The ninth saying (22:20a) is another promise from the risen Christ that he is coming soon.

The tenth saying (22:20b) is a response to the risen Christ that expresses the hope that he will indeed come soon. It echoes the Aramaic prayer "Maranatha" ("Our Lord, come") found at the end of 1 Corinthians (16:22; see also *Didache* 10:6). This is surely one of the oldest Christian prayers.

The book ends in 22:21 with a benediction that suggests that the book is to be read publicly in church services (see 1:3).

For Reflection: Christian life always has as its horizon the Lord's coming and the fullness of God's kingdom. We are expected to live as if the Lord's coming is imminent, and so we are to be prepared always for his coming. In this way we can regard the last judgment as a vindication rather than as a threat. This is common New Testament teaching. And yet after more than 1,900 years the Lord has not yet come in the ways that the book of Revelation expects. What do you make of this? How would you explain it to someone else?

For Further Study

Aune, D.E. *Revelation 1—5, 6—16, 17—22*, 3 vols. (Dallas: Word, 1997-99).

Bauckham, R. *The Theology of the Book of Revelation* (Cambridge, UK—New York: Cambridge University Press, 1993).

Boring, M. E. *Revelation* (Louisville: Westminster/Knox, 1989).

Charles, R. H. *A Critical and Exegetical Commentary on the Revelation of St. John* (New York: Scribners, 1920).

Corsini, E. *The Apocalypse. The Perennial Revelation of Jesus* (Wilmington: Glazier, 1983).

Giblin, C. H. *The Book of Revelation. The Open Book of Prophecy* (Collegeville, MN: Liturgical Press, 1991).

Harrington, W. J. *Revelation* (Collegeville, MN: Liturgical Press, 1993).

Hemer, C. J. *The Letters to the Seven Churches of Asia in their Local Setting* (Sheffield, UK: JSOT, 1986).

Kraybill, J. N. *Imperial Cult and Commerce in John's Apocalypse* (Sheffield, UK: Sheffield Academic Press, 1996).

Krodel, G. A. *Revelation* (Minneapolis: Augsburg, 1989).

Murphy, F.J. *Fallen Is Babylon: The Revelation to John* (Harrisburg, PA: Trinity Press International, 1998).

O'Leary, S. D. *Arguing the Apocalypse. A Theory of Millennial Rhetoric* (New York—Oxford: Oxford University Press, 1994).

Roloff, J. *The Revelation of John* (Minneapolis: Fortress, 1993).

Schüssler Fiorenza, E. *Revelation: Vision of a Just World* (Minneapolis: Fortress, 1991).

Thompson, L. L. *The Book of Revelation. Apocalypse and Empire* (New York: Oxford University Press, 1990).

Wainwright, A. W. *Mysterious Apocalypse. Interpreting the Book of Revelation* (Nashville: Abingdon, 1993).

Yarbro Collins, A. *Crisis and Catharsis. The Power of the Apocalypse* (Philadelphia: Fortress, 1984).